A
MOTHER'S
CRY

Sattamini de Arruda family. Front row, from left to right: Marcos, Monica (on floor), Lina, and Martinha; back row: Cristiana and Miguel. From family photo album.

LINA PENNA SATTAMINI

A
MOTHER'S
CRY

A Memoir of
Politics, Prison, and
Torture under the
Brazilian Military
Dictatorship

Edited and with   Translated by   Epilogue by
an Introduction by   Rex P. Nielson and   Marcos P. S.
James N. Green   James N. Green   Arruda

Duke University Press   Durham and London   2010

© 2010 Duke University Press,
originally published in Brazil in Portuguese
(Produtor Editorial Independente, 2000)

All rights reserved

Printed in the United States of America on acid-free paper ♾

Designed by Heather Hensley

Typeset in Adobe Jensen Pro by Tseng Information Systems, Inc.

Library of Congress Cataloging-in-Publication Data appear on
the last printed page of this book.

Marcos, Cristiana, Mônica, Lina, Miguel, Martinha,

and in memory of Marisa (1950†)

CONTENTS

ACKNOWLEDGMENTS

My eternal gratitude to:

Maria Penna Sattamini, my tireless mother, who saved Marcos's life by looking for him until he was found.

My children:

Marcos, for his steadfast courage and stoic patience;

Cristiana, for being our devoted contact in Washington, D.C., and our host when we arrived;

Miguel, for the letters and notes and all of his and his wife Lúcia's support before and after Marcos was freed;

Martinha, for her efforts in coordinating contacts, organizing our finances, and undertaking so much other work;

Mônica, who was so young, but didn't hesitate to give all of the comfort and love that was needed.

I am very proud to be the mother of all of you because with all of the pressure and the constant threats you didn't hesitate one moment and helped.

Clemildo Lyra de Arruda, Marcos's father, who joined my mother so many times in search of Marcos and accompanied her to the hospitals, and for the many letters that he sent to Marcos that were so encouraging;

Técio Lins e Silva, our fearless lawyer, one of a few who would accept such cases, who proved Marcos's innocence and demanded justice, and all without charging a fee;

Elza de Britto Pereira, my sister, who provided the means to get to the secretary of General-President Médici, and who on numerous occasions sought out people who could help us;

Colonel Octávio Medeiros, for having tried to speed up Marcos's transfer from São Paulo to Rio;

Jack Otero, my trade union friend in Washington, D.C., who gave me advice on what to do (and it worked);

Father Michael Colonnese, who did so much for us after I wrote him a letter and who even took Marcos to Rome to meet with Pope Paul VI;

Amnesty International, for giving Marcos the status of prisoner of conscience, and for the persistent work of a group of fourteen people in Philadelphia who wrote to government officials, the armed forces, and the courts;

Stanley D. Baurys, the leader of the Amnesty International group in Philadelphia, who had such a great influence in the case and who will be in our hearts forever;

Mr. Reardon, the U.S. Consul General, for having accompanied us on an unsuccessful visit, showing great interest in the case, and for helping us get a visa when we went to the United States;

Ms. Beulah Confer, who was a program officer for the U.S. Agency for International Development, and when I was in Rio de Janeiro kept me informed about the impact of our campaign to free Marcos;

Joe DeFonzo, for having gotten me so much work, so that I could earn money for our campaign, and for doing so much else for me;

Congressman Joel T. Broyhill, for helping speed up my naturalization case;

Ron Smith and *Tom Doherty*, for having been the sponsors for my naturalization;

Neil Seideman, who as my boss at the State Department helped with lots of work;

Bishop Dom Aloísio Lorscheider, who so graciously received and comforted us and asked Dom Alberto Trevisan, the Auxiliary Bishop of Rio de Janeiro, to visit Marcos, even though the military would not let him do so;

Mr. Malcolm Hallam, who was my boss when I worked in the U.S. Consulate in Rio de Janeiro and later was the Consul in São Paulo when he called the Consul in Rio and recommended that they help me;

Elizabeth and *Patrick French,* our friends since 1971, when they received Marcos with open arms and became part of our family and who even paid Marcos's tuition for a trimester at American University when he was without work;

Marcos's colleagues and teachers who signed a statement that he was never epileptic;

Professor James N. Green, for his commitment to make the dream of getting an English version of my book published and known in the United States;

Marycarolyn G. France and *Sophia Beal,* for their work in editing the English version of this project; and

Rex P. Nielson for the translation.

A POLITICAL CHRONOLOGY OF THE
BRAZILIAN MILITARY DICTATORSHIP, 1964–85

1960

APRIL President Juscelino Kubitschek inaugurates the new capital of Brasília.

OCTOBER Jânio Quadros is elected president.

1961

AUGUST President Quadros abruptly resigns. After overcoming objections by the armed forces, Vice-President João Goulart of the Brazilian Labor Party assumes the presidency with diminished powers.

1962

JUNE Students from the Catholic left form Ação Popular (Popular Action).

JULY In White House meetings with advisers on Latin America, President Kennedy indicates that he would support a military overthrow of the Goulart government.

OCTOBER During Brazilian congressional and gubernatorial elections, the U.S. Central Intelligence Agency (CIA) covertly channels money to candidates who oppose President Goulart.

1963

SEPTEMBER The journalist and governor of the state of Guanabara (Greater Rio de Janeiro) Carlos Lacerda defends a coup d'état against President Goulart.

1964

MARCH A massive demonstration in Rio de Janeiro supports Goulart's call for land reform and other progressive measures, while businessmen and the Catholic Church mobilize middle-class anticommunist sentiment against the leftwing program of the Goulart government.

<dl>
<dt>APRIL</dt>
<dd>A rebellion of the armed forces overthrows the government of President Goulart. President Lyndon B. Johnson immediately recognizes the new regime.</dd>
<dd>The military decrees an Institutional Act that expands the powers of the presidency and allows it to suspend the political rights of politicians.</dd>
<dd>Marshall Humberto Castello Branco, a four-star general, is elected president by a purged Congress.</dd>
<dt>JUNE</dt>
<dd>A purged Congress extends President Castello Branco's term in office until March 15, 1967.</dd>
</dl>

1965

<dl>
<dt>OCTOBER</dt>
<dd>Opposition candidates are elected as governors of the important states of Guanabara and Minas Gerais.</dd>
<dd>Castello Branco issues Institutional Act No. 2 that dissolves the political parties, establishes an official pro-government party and an "opposition" party, and creates an indirect election process for the president, vice-president, and governors.</dd>
</dl>

1966

<dl>
<dt>OCTOBER</dt>
<dd>The Congress elects four-star general Artur de Costa e Silva as the new president.</dd>
<dt>NOVEMBER</dt>
<dd>The former governor Carlos Lacerda organizes the Frente Ampla (Broad Front) in an attempt to unite ex-presidents Kubitschek, Quadros, and Goulart against the military regime.</dd>
</dl>

1967

<dl>
<dt>NOVEMBER</dt>
<dd>Carlos Marighella, a former leader of the Brazilian Communist Party, initiates an urban guerrilla campaign against the military regime. During the next five years over a dozen armed struggle groups will operate in Brazil.</dd>
</dl>

1968

<dl>
<dt>MARCH</dt>
<dd>The killing of high school student Edson Luís in Rio de Janeiro by police sparks a nationwide wave of student demonstrations against the military government.</dd>
<dt>APRIL-JUNE</dt>
<dd>The government outlaws Lacerda's Broad Front.</dd>
</dl>

The military represses wildcat strikes by workers in Minas Gerais and São Paulo.

OCTOBER   Military police arrest 920 student representatives and leaders in a national meeting of the National Union of Students.

DECEMBER   President Costa e Silva decrees Institutional Act No. 5 that closes Congress, suspends *habeas corpus*, expands press censorship, and takes away the political rights of many politicians for ten years.

1969

MAY   The military expels seventy prominent professors from the country's major universities for their alleged subversive activities.

SEPTEMBER Two revolutionary organizations kidnap the U.S. ambassador. He is freed after the military releases and flies to Mexico fifteen student and political leaders, who had been tortured while incarcerated.

OCTOBER   President Costa e Silva, who suffered a stroke in September, is replaced by four-star general Emílio Médici.

1970

MARCH   Pope Paul VI condemns the widespread torture of political prisoners in Brazil.

APRIL   The Latin American Studies Association (LASA) meeting in Washington, D.C., resolves to denounce torture in Brazil and calls on the U.S. government to cut off all economic and military aid to the dictatorship.

MAY   Marcos Arruda is arrested in São Paulo.

JUNE   The National Council of Churches and the U.S. Conference of Catholic Bishops present a dossier about torture in Brazil to the Inter-American Commission on Human Rights of the Organization of American States.

1971

FEBRUARY   Marcos Arruda is released from prison.

MAY   Senator Frank Church of Idaho conducts Congressional hearings about U.S. aid and support to the Brazilian police.

DECEMBER   The Committee against Repression in Brazil (CARIB) organizes protests in Washington, D.C., against the official visit of President Médici to the Nixon White House.

1972

SEPTEMBER   Amnesty International releases a list naming four hundred Brazilian officials known to be involved in the torture of political prisoners.

1973

JANUARY   Several urban guerrilla organizations issue a statement in an article in the French newspaper *Le Monde* recognizing the failure of the guerrilla strategy to overthrow the military government.

1974

JANUARY   Four-star general Ernesto Geisel is indirectly elected president.

NOVEMBER   The Brazilian Democratic Movement, the opposition political party, trounces the official government party in Congressional elections.

1975

OCTOBER   The television journalist Vladimir Herzog is detained and killed in São Paulo while being questioned about alleged membership in the Brazilian Communist Party. Over 8,000 people defy government restrictions and join an ecumenical religious ceremony in his memory.

1976

APRIL   Students strike throughout the country.

NOVEMBER   The opposition political party makes major gains in municipal elections.

1977

MAY   In protest against the arrest of student activists in São Paulo, 80,000 students go on strike throughout the country

SEPTEMBER   The police invade the Catholic University of São Paulo and arrest 1,700 students.

1978

MAY   Metalworkers in Greater São Paulo organize a wildcat strike, defying the military's economic and labor policies.

OCTOBER   João Figueiredo is selected as the fifth general to assume the presidency.

1979

AUGUST   The Congress approves an amnesty bill freeing most political prisoners and allowing most exiles to return to Brazil, but the law absolves all torturers of criminal prosecution.

1980

NOVEMBER The Congress passes a law reintroducing the direct election of governors.

1981

APRIL A bomb being planted by rightwing army intelligence officers accidentally explodes outside the Rio Center, where a fundraising concert for the opposition is taking place.

1982

Opposition candidates win the country's most important governorships and a majority in Congress.

1983

FEBRUARY A nationwide campaign begins to demand direct presidential elections, mobilizing millions throughout the country over the subsequent year.

1984

APRIL Pro-dictatorship forces in Congress defeat a constitutional amendment to establish direct presidential elections.

1985

JANUARY A coalition of opposition forces and dissident sectors of the progovernment party support Tancredo Neves for president and José Sarney for vice-president. They win a majority in the electoral college.

MARCH Sarney, who had previously supported the military government, temporarily assumes the presidency when Neves falls ill.

On Inauguration Day, President Figueiredo avoids the swearing in ceremony and leaves the presidential palace through a side door, marking the end of military rule.

APRIL Sarney becomes president on the death of President Neves, becoming the first civilian to rule the country since April 1964.

THE PERSONAL AND THE POLITICAL UNDER
THE BRAZILIAN MILITARY REGIME

This is a story about a mother's love for her son. It is about how a family united to save the life of a brother, a nephew, a grandson. It also tells about the suffering of one of the thousands of Brazilians who dared to challenge the military regime that came to power on March 31, 1964, and only relinquished control of the State two decades later.[1]

In the years since the generals returned to their military posts in 1985, dozens of participants who vigorously opposed the Brazilian dictatorship have published memoirs about their activities.[2] They have written about their experiences in the legal political opposition, in the student movement, and in armed actions against the state, and about their lives underground and in exile. Human rights groups and victims of the generals' arbitrary rule have published accounts of those who disappeared after being arrested and were buried in unmarked graves. Scholars have combed through archives to reconstruct the histories of leftwing organizations that operated clandestinely and carried out activities against the dictatorship. Journalists and historians have analyzed the nature of the authoritarian regime, detailing the internal politics of the military governments and explaining the rise and fall of the generals' rule.[3]

As Brazilian academics and former political actors evaluated the country's recent history, pressure mounted in the 1990s to demand that the government offer indemnities for those who had been wrongly blacklisted, imprisoned, tortured, and otherwise abused. At the same time, some prominent intellectuals and politicians began to assert that Brazilians should turn the page on this tragic chapter of Brazilian history. After all, some argued, the military had negotiated an Amnesty Law in 1979 that had allowed exiles to return to the country and had freed most political prisoners. It was simply time to forget the past and move on.

Lina Penna Sattamini, however, could not forget. The military arrested her son Marcos Arruda in May 1970. He almost died under torture. Moreover, the Amnesty Law of 1979 had also absolved all torturers of any criminal liability. Those who had harmed her son would not be prosecuted. Her rage at this call for amnesia in the wake of an amnesty that also included impunity for those who had tortured detainees drove her to write an intensely emotional and powerful testimony to those times. *Esquecer? Nunca Mais* . . . [Forget? Never Again . . .] is the saga of her son's ordeal. It was originally published in 2000 by a small Brazilian press.[4] Her story captures the intimate personal dramas of the friends and family of Marcos Arruda, a young geologist turned industrial worker who opted to confront the State and the economic system that it defended in an attempt to bring down the dictatorship and transform Brazilian society.

For those unfamiliar with the history of the Brazilian military dictatorship, a brief account of the political, economic, and social events of the second half of the twentieth century is in order. It will provide a context for Lina Penna Sattamini's memoir about the arrest and torture of her son, the prolonged effort to release him, and his exile to the United States.

In the 1960s, the Arruda family had become transnational. Lina Sattamini had gone through a difficult separation from her husband, so she decided to move to the United States to find a degree of personal and economic independence. She worked hard to maintain family unity from afar, encouraging her children to visit the United States and live there for a time. She also maintained intimate links with relatives and friends in Brazil. Over time, her family, like the two nations, developed a close and complex relationship.

The United States was the first country to recognize independent Brazil in 1824. In the nineteenth century, American consumers' growing preference for coffee helped fuel a boom in Brazil's most important export crop. By the beginning of the twentieth century, trading ties had bound the two nations closely together. Brazil sided with the Allies during the Second World War and deployed troops to Italy to fight against the Axis powers. As a mark of this "special relationship," the U.S. government established naval bases in Brazil as part of the war effort and helped set up the country's steel industry at the end of the war. Throughout the century, U.S. cultural, economic, and political influence in Brazil deepened. Hollywood movies and U.S. consumer goods—from comic books to cars—became common. U.S. investments in the country grew as well. Close military relations that were cemented during the Second World War continued as the Cold War set in. U.S. policymakers sought to build a strong alliance with Brazil as a means of preventing communist or radical nationalist governments from coming to power in that country or others throughout Latin America.

In the 1950s, presidents Getúlio Vargas (1951–54) and Juscelino Kubitschek (1955–60) promised economic development, modernization, and greater distribution of the country's wealth.[5] Vargas had a long political career. He first came to the presidency as a reformer in 1930, but then took on dictatorial powers in 1937. He supported the United States in the Second World War but was pushed out of office by the military in 1945. He returned to the presidency in 1951 and rebuilt his political fortunes in the 1950s with support from leftwing trade unions, nationalists, and those who believed that the State should play an active role in solving Brazil's economic and social problems. During his presidency, for example, the government nationalized the oil industry. Pressured to leave office by sectors of the armed forces, Vargas committed suicide in the presidential palace in August 1954.

Vargas's successor, Juscelino Kubitschek, was more moderate. He believed that the country's economic development depended on government support, yet he also encouraged private and foreign investment. Kubitschek promised that during his administration Brazil would leap fifty years forward in five. His pet project was building a new capital in the country's interior. The inauguration of Brasília in 1960 with its modernist structures and optimistic urban planning projected the image of Brazil as a country on the move toward fulfilling its destiny of becoming a great power.

During the early 1960s, a surge in grassroots activism brought new actors onto the political stage. Leftwing students and labor unions mobilized to demand that the government nationalize foreign electric power companies. This campaign represented a larger nationalist sentiment in favor of State control of key national resources, increased industrialization, and other forms of economic development. In northeastern Brazil, peasants began organizing for land reform. Trade unions pushed to establish a national labor federation and carried out a series of strikes in favor of economic and political demands.[6] Students became more politically engaged. On the whole their ideological allegiances shifted toward the left and Marxist ideas. Overall, the political climate favored nationalist and leftwing populist politicians. These social and political movements in the early 1960s portended greater political participation by the dispossessed and greater pressure for a broader distribution of wealth to diminish a noticeable poverty gap.

During President Eisenhower's administration in the United States (1953–60), the U.S. State Department promoted trade over aid as the best strategy for Brazil's and other nations' progress. The Cuban revolution of 1959, however, alarmed U.S. policymakers. They feared that ongoing economic and social inequality, radicalizing urban and rural movements, and a leftwing presence among unionists in key sectors of the economy might create the conditions for a similar social upheaval in Brazil.[7]

Soon after taking office, President Kennedy (1961–63) announced a bold new aid program for Latin America, known as the Alliance for Progress. It promised to encourage reforms by addressing the region's social and economic problems. Social aid programs designed to alleviate poverty, controlled land reform that would distribute some land to peasants, and technical aid to rural cooperatives and urban unions were among the strategies designed to stem growing communist influence in Latin America and the Caribbean, or so Washington policymakers thought. If reasonable reforms could take place under the guidance of the United States Agency for International Development (USAID) and other assistance programs, then revolutions might be averted.[8] Increased aid and training of the military and the police would also provide the necessary tools to quell any insurrections that might threaten moderate change.[9] The Kennedy administration targeted Brazil as a priority for the Alliance for Progress program and sent Harvard-educated economist Lincoln Gordon, one of the architects of the plan, to Rio de Janeiro as its ambassador.

Meanwhile, an unforeseen turn of events in 1961 changed Brazil's political landscape. Jânio Quadros, a rightwing populist and former governor of the state of São Paulo, succeeded Kubitschek as president in January 1961. He had campaigned on a platform to sweep out corruption from the federal government. Quadros was a maverick politician, and he came to power without strong political support from the country's three major political parties. He turned out to be an erratic politician, who became frustrated when he could not get a majority in Congress to back his policies.

Then, in August 1961 he suddenly resigned from office. Most historians agree that he took this drastic measure as a way of pressuring Congress to clamor for his return to office in exchange for increased presidential authority and political support. Those demands for his return never materialized, and so the presidency went to João Goulart, the former minister of labor during the Vargas government and vice-president under the centrist government of Kubitshek and the right-leaning administration of Quadros. Goulart was a leader of the center-left Brazilian Labor Party (PTB). He was elected vice-president in 1956 and again in 1961 because Brazilian law allowed voters to split their ticket. When Quadros resigned, a sector of the military tried to block Goulart's succession. After other members of the armed forces threatened a civil war, he was allowed to assume office, but with reduced powers. Suddenly, a politician sympathetic to the left was in the presidential palace, which worried U.S. policymakers, rightwing Brazilian politicians, the upper echelons of the Catholic Church, business leaders, and conservative members of the armed forces. Would Goulart lead the country toward radical reforms or even revolution?

Overnight, Brazil became the center of geopolitical anxieties spurred on by Cold War ideologies. To the U.S. State Department, important figures in the Brazilian Catholic Church, and rightwing politicians, Goulart was too sympathetic to the left. As a leader of the Brazilian Labor Party, he had, in fact, built his support from unions, including forging occasional alliances with members of the Brazilian Communist Party. But, he was also a large-scale landowner from southern Brazil. In a White House meeting between former President Kubitschek and President Kennedy held on September 15, 1961, the Brazilian politician reassured Kennedy that Goulart was *not* a radical.[10] Washington policymakers were not convinced.

During Goulart's presidency (1961–64), social and political polarization deepened. Peasant organizations demanded land redistribution.[11] At the same time, labor unions carried out a series of strikes to offset falling wages due to increasing inflation. University students enthusiastically supported these popular mobilizations and pushed for radical change. Different political forces called for national control over mineral resources and development policies that would address longstanding poverty and inequality.

Many turned to Marxism as an ideology and to Cuba as a model for social transformation.[12]

Military officers, already alarmed by Goulart's left-leaning politics, became particularly concerned when rank-and-file soldiers and sailors mobilized to force democratic reforms within the armed forces. They sought to form unions that, among other demands, would allow them to study during off-duty hours, wear civilian clothes when on leave, and run as candidates in elections. Large-scale landowners panicked when peasant leagues occupied their land and demanded that the state intervene and redistribute it to the landless. Large portions of the Brazilian middle classes and significant sectors of the Catholic Church feared that Goulart's alliances with the Communist Party might lead to a socialist revolution.[13] Moreover, excessive government spending during the Kubitschek years to build the new capital combined with government subsidies for basic goods and services caused a large budget deficit. Goulart's solution was to print more money, which produced inflation. Price hikes worried consumers who were apprehensive that Goulart had lost control of the economy.

In 1962, President Kennedy decided that if the military overthrew Goulart, his administration would support the effort. The U.S. ambassador Lincoln Gordon and his military attaché Vernon Walters kept in close contact with leaders of the armed forces who favored deposing the president. They assured those conspiring to topple the Goulart government that the United States would back a coup d'état. After Kennedy's assassination in November 1963, President Lyndon B. Johnson (1963–68) continued the same pro-coup policy.[14]

On March 31, 1964, army units from the state of Minas Gerais rose up against the central government. On April 1, the majority of the armed forces declared their support for Goulart's ouster. The United States government sent a naval detachment to provide logistical support for the rebellion should a civil war break out. The clandestine deployment known as "Operation Brother Sam" was unnecessary, as the Brazilian generals quickly took power.[15] President Johnson immediately recognized the new military government. Goulart sought political asylum in Uruguay.

Less than a week later, a purged Brazilian Congress passed the presidency to General Castello Branco, which he held until 1967. President Johnson authorized foreign aid and loans to shore up Brazil's faltering economy.

In order to retain international and domestic legitimacy, the generals maintained political institutions, including the Congress and political parties. Yet, they granted themselves supreme power to issue degrees and institutional acts when necessary to ensure absolute control over the people, the government, and the State.

The military takeover of 1964 also opened Brazil to greater foreign investments. Transnational corporations headquartered in the United States expanded their operations in the country. The new regime scrapped a profit remittance law passed under Goulart's governance. (Designed to limit large-scale capital outflow, it had required that foreign companies reinvest a percentage of their profits in the country.) The new military government also clamped down on militant labor activists. Many leftwing leaders—communists, socialists, and Labor Party supporters—were purged from top posts in labor unions and federations. The government imposed tighter control over unions. It placed strict limitations on the right to strike and created a "favorable investment climate" for foreign companies. From 1968 to 1978 labor unrest was virtually nonexistent.

Many who opposed Goulart's government assumed that the military would step in, clean house, and then retreat to the barracks. That, however, was not the case. During two decades of the dictatorship's rule, every time significant legal opposition to the military mounted, the generals changed the rules of the game. They took away opposition politicians' political rights. They closed down Congress. They censored the press. When threatened, they employed heavy-handed measures to stay in power. In order to enact their policies, the generals issued a series of Institutional Acts that overrode the constitution. This enabled them to rule at will. In October 1965, when the opposition candidates for the governorship of the states of Minas Gerais and Guanabara (Greater Rio de Janeiro) defeated the pro-government candidates, the military decreed Institutional Act No. 2 that dissolved all political parties. Instead it created an official pro-government party and an official opposition political party.

In this regard, the Brazilian military dictatorship seems different from other authoritarian regimes that came to power in Latin America in the 1960s and '70s. Brazilian military rulers built a governing alliance with rightwing politicians, large-scale landowners, and the captains of industry. They sought support among the middle class and conservative sectors of the

Catholic Church, and they were concerned about their legitimacy. Therefore, they did not abolish elections or political parties. Rather they carefully controlled the political process to ensure that they stayed in power by utilizing the formal institutions of democracy, when it served their interests. When it got in the way, they ignored democratic rights and procedures.

In 1967 and 1968, diverse political and social sectors coalesced in opposition to the military regime. Carlos Lacerda, the former governor of the state of Guanabara, who had been an outspoken opponent of the Goulart government, became frustrated that his presidential aspirations had been foiled. He broke with the dictatorship, and then worked to form a political coalition, known as the *Frente Ampla* (Broad Front) to unite former presidents Kubitschek, Quadros, and Goulart against the military regime. (The military outlawed this attempted alliance in April 1968.) Members of the opposition political party, the Brazilian Democratic Movement, spoke out in Congress against the military regime. Students also came to the forefront in their opposition to the dictatorship. They mobilized against the military's educational policies. When military police killed Edson Luís, a high school student living in Rio de Janeiro, during a demonstration in March 1968, protests broke out throughout the country. On June 26, 1968, 100,000 people participated in a march through downtown Rio de Janeiro calling for an end to military rule.[16]

At the same time, tens of thousands of youth turned to leftwing organizations to channel political discontent. Some groups defended the necessity of following Cuban or Chinese revolutionary models by organizing rural or urban guerrilla movements to challenge and eventually overthrow the military dictatorship. Other groups argued that it was essential to conduct patient grassroots organizing in order to forge close links with the industrial working class or with peasants in the countryside as part of a strategic plan to mobilize against military rule.

Among the thousands of Brazilian youth who joined the opposition to the military regime was Marcos Arruda. As a geology student and university activist, he became increasing radicalized after the military took power in 1964. He eventually joined one of the leftwing groups, known as *Ação Popular* (Popular Action) that was organizing against the military regime. Ação Popular was founded in 1962 by Catholic youth who sought to link their Christian beliefs with an involvement in political activities to solve the social and economic problems of the country. As the political situation worsened after the military took power in 1964, Ação Popular turned to Marxism as a theoretical framework to understand and change Brazilian society. After a long process of political maturation detailed in this book's epilogue, Arruda decided to follow the political orientation of Ação Popular and take a job in a factory. He found work in a plant in the industrial belt around São Paulo. His and his colleagues' goals were to labor side by side with the low-wage earners in the most dynamic sector of the economy in order to raise their fellow workers' consciousness about the political situation in the country. Ação Popular militants considered this to be a crucial first step in a larger strategy to overthrow military rule and reorganize the Brazilian economy and social structure.

Others chose different paths in opposing the military regime. Fidel Castro and his band of bearded revolutionaries that had overthrown the Cuban dictatorship of Fulgencio Batista served as their blueprint. Many students and other opponents of the regime thought that Brazil's situation was comparable to that of Cuba, so they formed or joined underground guerrilla organizations.[17] To cite one example, Carlos Marighella, a former leader of the Brazilian Communist Party, broke with that organization in 1967 after a trip to Cuba, and founded Ação Libertadora Nacional (National Liberating Action). Their strategy to overthrow the military government involved organizing armed units that "expropriated" money from banks and arms from military installations in order to sustain their organizations and accumulate resources to establish rural guerrilla bases. When they were prepared to move to the countryside, they planned to carry out guerrilla operations that would lead, so they thought, to large-scale confrontations with the military. They envisioned that their actions would inspire others to rise up and overthrow the military regime.[18]

Only a small minority of the students who joined legal demonstrations against the military government in 1968 became members of these guerrilla organizations that, for a time, enjoyed sympathy among many Brazilian youth because of a seeming willingness to take drastic actions and make great sacrifices to end military rule.[19]

Other student activists and leaders, such as Marcos Arruda, disagreed with this approach. Rather than prepare for military confrontations with the regime, they believed that it was more important to organize grassroots support among industrial workers. As Marxists they firmly believed that the working class would play a critical role in any major transformation of Brazilian society, including the overthrow of the military dictatorship.

The generals' response to all of the regime's radical opponents was political repression. In the immediate aftermath of the 1964 military coup d'état, the government targeted any political activists who seemed to oppose its rule. It used torture to extract information from those who organized against the dictatorship. Torture not only supplied the government with information about clandestine operations but also engendered fear among the leftwing activists and their supporters.

Throughout 1968, opposition to the military government mounted. A wave of student protests swept the country. The legal opposition became more outspoken in its objections to the military dictatorship.[20] Politicians took to the floor of Congress and denounced the government's repression of student demonstrations and the use of torture. Sectors of the Catholic Church began to speak out against the military regime and support student protests.[21] Wildcat strikes took place in two of the country's industrial centers. In October, a thousand students held a clandestine meeting of the National Union of Students. The police surrounded the farm where the national gathering was taking place and arrested the delegates and leaders. Then, on December 13, 1968, the military initiated a crackdown. A government decree, known as Institutional Act No. 5, closed Congress, suspended habeas corpus, expanded censorship, and shelved other democratic protections.

A wave of arrests ensued. Torture became widespread and systematic. Police and military officers assumed that anyone implicated in or supportive of anti-government activities was guilty until proven innocent. Upon arrest, the military and the police immediately tortured most detainees to extract details about the identity, whereabouts, and activities of other members or supporters of a given leftwing political organization. Few who were arrested after 1968 were spared these methods. Many died while being interrogated. Marcos Arruda's treatment, described so vividly by his mother and in his own recollections of those horrific months in prison, was the norm.[22]

In response to this intensification of repression, throughout Brazil small disparate groups of leftists, Catholic and Protestant clergy, intellectuals, journalists, and activists initiated campaigns to denounce the use of torture against political prisoners.[23] They collected statements and documented the government's abuse of political prisoners. They sought international support for their cause and relied on allies in the Catholic Church, as well as liberal and progressive forces in the United States and Europe, to come to their assistance.[24]

In June 1970, representatives of the U.S.-based National Council of Churches of Christ, an ecumenical coalition of Protestant denominations, and the U.S. Conference of Catholic Bishops turned over a thick dossier to the General Secretary of the Inter-American Commission on Human Rights (IACHR) of the Organization of America States in Washington, D.C. It contained detailed descriptions of the systematic use of torture on Brazilian political prisoners based on firsthand accounts smuggled out of Brazil and compiled into a comprehensive report. After reading the extensive documentation, one could not doubt the veracity of the denunciations. At the same time, scholars of Latin America working in the United States circulated petitions and passed resolutions demanding that the Brazilian government end the practice of political imprisonment and that the U.S. government cut off all aid to the military regime. These detailed allegations of human rights abuses eventually caught the attention of the mainstream press and members of the U.S. Congress.[25]

Until the 1968 crackdown, U.S. politicians and the media had, by and large, echoed State Department officials that publicly registered some reservations about the limits to democracy in Brazil but were hesitant to take a strong stand against the generals in charge. The consistent and persistent reports about torture awakened wider concern about the conditions of human rights in Brazil. Senator Frank Church (Democrat, Idaho) held a closed session hearing in May 1971 on U.S. government support of police programs in Brazil.[26] Church later issued a blasting critique of misguided U.S. foreign aid policy that gave economic and political support to an authoritarian regime. While these international campaigns sought to alleviate the pain and suffering of Brazilian political prisoners, thousands lingered in jails.

After a long and arduous campaign, Marcos Arruda's family and friends managed to get him released from prison in 1971. Fearful that he would be rearrested and once again submitted to torture, Arruda left the country. He arrived in Washington, D.C., soon after the Senate hearing on U.S. aid to

Brazil. Through a contact at the U.S. Conference of Catholic Bishops, which generously offered him a job soon after his arrival, he made contacts with the press. Dan Griffin, a journalist who had lived in Brazil, interviewed Arruda for the *Washington Post*. Griffin then published a full-length feature article entitled "The Torture of a Brazilian" that described Arruda's prison ordeal in gripping detail.[27] It was the first time that such a meticulous account of torture of a Latin American activist by his or her government had appeared in the U.S. press. The story provoked a hard-hitting *Washington Post* editorial against President Richard M. Nixon's support for the Brazilian regime.[28] The news item and accompanying editorial also reinforced the growing sentiment on opinion pages of U.S. newspapers that Washington should not be directing its foreign aid to repressive regimes.

Three years later, a Congressional hearing documented the arrest and torture of Fred Morris, a U.S. Methodist minister living in Brazil.[29] In 1975, the Harkin Amendment to the Foreign Assistance Act gave Congress the power to limit U.S. economic assistance to "any country which engages in a consistent pattern of gross violations of internationally recognized human rights."[30] The following year, Congress expanded this restriction to include military aid.

In 1973, representatives of several revolutionary organizations living in Paris declared that the guerrilla strategy had failed. Most of the guerrilla organizations had been crushed through systematic government campaigns. Having mopped up the last remnants of the armed-struggle organizations, the repressive apparatus then moved against the Brazilian Communist Party that had ironically adopted a moderate strategy in opposing the military regime. In 1975, the police arrested Vladimir Herzog, a São Paulo television journalist, and alleged member of the Communist Party. He died during interrogation, but the police insisted that he had hanged himself while in custody. Over 8,000 people defied government restrictions and attended an ecumenical religious service in his memory at the Catholic cathedral in downtown São Paulo. It was the largest public protest against the military regime since 1968.

When Ernesto Geisel came to power in 1974 as the fourth four-star general to rule the country, he promised a gradual move toward liberalization and an eventual return to democracy. "Political decompression," as it was called, included lifting some restrictions on election campaigning. To the military's chagrin, the opposition Brazilian Democratic Movement trounced the official pro-government party in that year's Congressional races. At the same time, economic woes, fueled by the international oil crisis of the 1970s, weakened the military's support among the middle class. As Geisel navigated the political system toward a controlled democratization, the opposition gained ground. The Brazilian Democratic Movement continued to outpoll the military in municipal and national Congressional elections. In 1976 and 1977, students began protesting the repressive nature of the military regime. The following year, industrial workers from the automobile industries in the Greater São Paulo area went out on strike against the government's restrictive wage policies.

During Marcos Arruda's sojourn in the United States, he played a leadership role in building national campaigns against U.S. government support for the authoritarian regimes in Brazil, Chile, Argentina, and other Latin American countries. He later moved to Europe to continue work related to human rights and social justice, collaborating with the internationally renowned Brazilian educator Paulo Freire and other Brazilian exiles at the Instituto de Ação Cultural (Institute of Cultural Action) in Geneva, Switzerland. He joined an educational project in Guinea Bissau, a small African nation that had recently achieved independence from Portuguese colonial rule. Arruda also participated in the production of a widely circulated book about Brazilian exiles, designed to support the campaign for a political amnesty and the return of those activists forced to live abroad.[31]

In 1979, after a vigorous campaign by the Brazilian opposition, João Figueiredo, the fifth four-star general to assume the presidency, granted amnesty to most political prisoners and exiles. Marcos Arruda returned to Brazil briefly and then resettled permanently in his homeland in 1982. He has continued to be involved in political action, intellectual production, and grassroots organizations working to build an alternative world of social equality and justice.[32] His mother, Lina, likewise returned to Brazil, in 1981, where she worked as an interpreter until she retired.

When Lina Sattamini's rage at those who wanted to forget the stories of torture victims propelled her to write her own memoir about the saga of her son, she had a wealth of letters and other material at her disposal to document her account. Because she had been in the United States when her son was arrested and needed to continue working there to raise funds to support the campaign to get him released from prison, she and her family ended up producing a trove of correspondences. These letters document their day-to-day agony as they tried to locate Marcos, look after his health, and finally free him. At the time, international telephone calls were expensive and complicated, so letters were the only economical means of communication. Had the family operated in Brazil alone, they likely would have destroyed any written records for fear of a possible police sweep of their homes. Fortunately, the letters were saved. Lina Sattamini's narrative captures her deep-felt tenderness, passion, love, and outrage. The family's heartfelt correspondences offer new generations of readers who live in decades distant from those times a powerful first-person account of how people coped with such an unbearable personal drama.

U.S. policymakers in Washington were slow to distance themselves from the Brazilian military dictatorship. President Nixon (1969–74) toasted four-star general and President Médici (1969–73) in the White House in December 1971. Marcos Arruda, Lina Sattamini, and their U.S. friends and allies protested the Brazilian dictator's visit in a small demonstration across the street in Lafayette Park. It took several years of campaigning and a broad coalition of liberal and progressive forces to convince Congress to force Gerald Ford's administration (1974–76) to take into account human rights when authorizing aid to foreign countries. U.S. policy to Brazil shifted significantly only when President Jimmy Carter (1977–1980) took office and prioritized human rights standards in foreign policy considerations.[33] By then, human rights had become a household term in the United States, and Amnesty International had been recognized as a world leader in the campaign against the use of torture. Lina Penna Sattamini's call that we must never forget is not merely a convocation to remember the past. It is also an appeal to denounce the ongoing uses of those techniques of interrogation that almost took her son's life.[34]

Notes

1. The references in this introduction are designed to offer the reader a pathway into the history of the Brazilian military dictatorship by citing the most important works in English. It is by no means exhaustive but should serve as a starting point for anyone wishing to learn more about this period.

2. Few of these memoirs have been translated into English. One, *A Grain of Mus-*

tard Seed: *The Awakening of the Brazilian Revolution,* is by Márcio Moreira Alves, a journalist and opposition politician, who was involved in the domestic and international campaign against torture in Brazil. Another, *Tropical Truth: A Story of Music and Revolution in Brazil,* is by singer and songwriter Caetano Veloso, who was imprisoned for a short time in the late 1960s and then left Brazil for a brief exile. The playwright and theater director Augusto Boal tells the story of his arrest and torture in *Hamlet and the Baker's Son: My Life in Theatre and Politics.* Translated by Adrian Jackson and Candida Blaker (London: Routledge, 2001).

3. The two most comprehensive English-language histories of Brazil under military rule are Maria Helena Moreira Alves, *State and Opposition in Military Brazil* (Austin: University of Texas Press, 1985) and Thomas E. Skidmore, *The Politics of Military Rule in Brazil, 1964–85* (New York: Oxford University Press, 1988).

4. Lina Penna Sattamini, *Esquecer? Nunca mais . . . (A saga do meu filho Marcos P. S. de Arruda)* (Rio de Janeiro: Produtor Independente, 2000).

5. Thomas E. Skidmore, *Politics in Brazil, 1930–1964: An Experiment in Democracy* (2nd ed.; New York: Oxford University Press, 2007); W. Michael Weis, *Cold Warriors and Coups D'état: Brazilian-American Relations, 1945–64* (Albuquerque: University of New Mexico Press, 1993).

6. Kenneth Paul Erickson, *The Brazilian Corporative State and Working Class Politics.* (Berkeley: University of California Press, 1977).

7. Stephen G. Rabe, *Eisenhower and Latin America: The Foreign Policy of Anti-Communism* (Chapel Hill: University of North Carolina Press, 1988).

8. Stephen G. Rabe, *The Most Dangerous Area in the World: John F. Kennedy Confronts Communist Revolution in Latin America* (Chapel Hill: University of North Carolina Press, 1999).

9. Martha K. Huggins, *Political Policing: The United States and Latin America* (Durham: Duke University Press, 1998).

10. Memorandum of Conversation between President Kennedy and Senator (former President) Kubitschek of Brazil, September 15, 1961, NSF, Box 12, Br. Gen. 10/61/–11/61, 1, John F. Kennedy Library.

11. Joseph A. Page, *The Revolution that Never Was: Northeast Brazil: 1955–1964* (New York: Grossman, 1972); Anthony W. Pereira, *The End of the Peasantry: The Rural Labor Movement in Northeast Brazil, 1961–1988* (Pittsburgh: University of Pittsburgh Press, 1997).

12. Jean Marc von der Weid, *Brazil, 1964 to the Present: A Political Analysis, an Interview with Jean Marc von der Weid* (Montreal: Latin American Editions, 1972).

13. The *Reader's Digest* published an account about the overthrow of the Goulart government that emphasizes the role of anticommunist forces, including the

conservative wing of the Catholic Church, in the events taking place in Brazil in the early 1960s. Clarence W. Hall, "The Country that Saved Itself," *Reader's Digest* 85 (November 1964): 135–59.

14. Jan Knippers Black, *United States Penetration of Brazil* (Philadelphia: University of Pennsylvania Press, 1977); Ruth Leacock, *Requiem for Revolution, The United States and Brazil, 1961–1969* (Kent, Ohio: Kent State University Press, 1990).

15. Phyllis R. Parker, *Brazil and the Quiet Intervention, 1964* (Austin: University of Texas Press, 1979).

16. Victoria Ann Langland, "Speaking of Flowers: Student Movements and Collective Memory in Authoritarian Brazil." Ph.D. diss. Yale University, 2004.

17. João Quartim, *Dictatorship and Armed Struggle in Brazil* (London: New Left Books, 1971).

18. Carlos Marighella. *For the Liberation of Brazil* (Middlesex: Penguin Books, 1971).

19. For example, in September 1969 two revolutionary organizations kidnapped the U.S. ambassador to Brazil and demanded the release of fifteen political prisoners in exchange for his freedom. Those who followed politics knew that political prisoners were being severely mistreated while in jail, and many cheered when the small band of rebels managed to seize the diplomatic representative of the most powerful foreign backer of the military regime. This event has been recreated in the Brazilian film *Four Days in September* (1997) directed by Bruno Barreto that was nominated for an Oscar as best foreign film.

20. Maria D'Alva Gil Kinzo, *Legal Opposition Politics under Authoritarian Rule in Brazil* (New York: St. Martin's Press, 1988).

21. Kenneth P. Serbin, *Secret Dialogues: Church-State Relations, Torture, and Social Justice in Authoritarian Brazil* (Pittsburgh: University of Pittsburgh Press, 2000).

22. Archdiocese of São Paulo, *Torture in Brazil*. Translated by Jaime Wright. Edited and with an Introduction by Joan Dassin (1st ed., 1986; Austin: University of Texas Press, 1998). Martha K. Huggins, Mika Haritos-Fatouros, and Philip G. Zimbardo. *Violence Workers: Police Torturers and Murderers Reconstruct Brazilian Atrocities* (Berkeley: University of California Press, 2002).

23. James N. Green, *We Cannot Remain Silent: Opposition to the Brazilian Dictatorship in the United States* (Durham: Duke University Press, 2010).

24. See, for example, Ralph Della Cava, "Torture in Brazil," *Commonweal* 62, no. 6 (April 24, 1970): 135–41; and "Reply," *Commonweal* 62, no. 14 (August 7, 1970), 378–79, 398–99.

25. Amnesty International, *Report on Allegations of Torture in Brazil* (Palo Alto: West Coast Office, Amnesty International, 1973).

26. U.S. Senate Subcommittee on Western Hemisphere Affairs, *United States Policies and Programs in Brazil: Hearing before the Subcommittee on Western Hemisphere Affairs of the Committee on Foreign Relations.* 92nd Cong. 1st sess. (May 4, 5, 11, 1971).

27. Dan Griffin, "The Torture of a Brazilian," *Washington Post* (September 19, 1971): D3-1.

28. Editorial, "Brazil and Torture," *Washington Post* (September 26, 1971): E-6.

29. U.S. Congress, Subcommittee on International Organizations and Movements of the Committee on Foreign Affairs, *Torture and Oppression in Brazil.* 93rd Cong., 2nd sess., (December 11, 1974). Fred B. Morris, "In the Presence of Mine Enemies." *Ramparts* (October 1975): 57-70.

30. Cited in Amalia Bartoli, Roger Burback, David Hathaway, Robert High, and Eugene Kelly, "Human Rights . . . 'In the Soul of Our Foreign Policy,'" NACLA *Report on the Americas* 3, no. 1 (March–April 1979): 4–11.

31. Pedro Celso Uchôa Calvacante and Jovelino Ramos, eds., *Mémorias do exílio, Brasil 1964–197?* (Lisbon: Arcádia, 1976; São Paulo: Editora e Livraria Livramento, 1978).

32. Among the books written or edited by Arruda are Marcos Arruda, *Transnational Corporations: A Challenge for Churches and Christians* (Geneva: Commission on the Churches' Participation in Development, World Council of Churches, 1982); John Cavanagh, Daphne Wysham, and Marcos Arruda, *Beyond Bretton Woods: Alternatives to the Global Economic Order* (London; Boulder: Pluto Press; Washington, D.C.: Institute for Policy Studies; Amsterdam: Transnational Institute, 1994); and Marcos Arruda, *External Debt: Brazil and the International Financial Crisis.* Translated by Peter Lenny (London; Boulder: Pluto Press in association with Christian Aid and the Transnational Institute, 2000).

33. Timothy J. Power, "Brazil and the Carter Human Rights Policy, 1977–1979," M.A. thesis, University of Florida, 1986.

34. In order to distinguish between the text of the documents that Lina Penna Sattamini quotes in her memoir and her own comments, we have bracketed her words, followed by the notation LPS. Other bracketed comments are those of the editor or the translator and are noted as such.

A Memoir

WE MUST
NEVER
FORGET

Lina Penna Sattamini

TRANSLATED BY

Rex P. Nielson and James N. Green

New York, May 20, 1970

I had just come back to the Statler Hilton in New York and asked for the key when I found the letter from my mother. My heart stopped. Marcos had been arrested! What else could this letter addressed to my hotel mean?

I had been working in the United States since 1958 as an interpreter for USAID (Agency for International Development). Technically I was called an escort-interpreter since I accompanied people for the organization wherever it was carrying out its projects.

Immediately, I called my mother in Rio de Janeiro who confirmed, "It's true. Marcos has been missing since the beginning of May. They say he was on his way to meet someone when they picked him up. We've just found out through a note from the General."

The source of our information, the General, was the father-in-law of my nephew, who is also my godson.

That's how it began, the true *Via Dolorosa* (Way of Suffering)* of our lives, a time of pain, desperation, and anger.

Someone provided him with the false information that Marcos had not yet been interrogated. That lie hid a terrible truth. My son had been tortured so badly that he had been taken to a hospital, where they thought he was going to die.

Marcos Penna Sattamini de Arruda was kidnapped in the middle of a street in São Paulo, on May 11, 1970, on his way to meet a woman for lunch. There wasn't the slightest record of his imprisonment anywhere. Marcos simply disappeared for twenty-four days.

Even before the note from the General reached our family, a friend of

---

* *Editor's note.* The *Via Dolorosa* (Way of Suffering) is the path that Jesus took on his way through Jerusalem to his crucifixion.

my daughter Martinha had telephoned. She told Martinha about Marcos's arrest and asked her to come to São Paulo.

Without telling anyone for fear of unnecessarily worrying her family, Martinha went to the home of Marcos's ex-wife in São Paulo looking for news of her brother. My ex-daughter-in-law would only open the door a crack. In a dismissive voice, she whispered, "Go back to Rio, Martinha. Forget Marcos."

Martinha insisted, "But he's been arrested. We have to try to find him."

Marcos's ex-wife simply closed the door.

Shocked and upset, my daughter stayed with a friend of her boyfriend's, saying that she was in town on business. The next day Martinha met with the friend who had phoned her about Marcos. She gave Martinha some advice about what the family should do to keep Marcos from being killed.

Meanwhile, my mother and others in Rio began to contact each and every member of the military that they or their friends knew. They eventually met with the minister of the army, who *promised Marcos wouldn't be touched . . .* a lie.

During the twenty-four days he was missing, my mother and Marcos's father, my ex-husband, went to every governmental agency they thought might be involved: DOPS [the Department of Social and Political Order], OBAN [Operation Bandeirantes], and the Tiradentes Prison in São Paulo.* They consistently heard the same denials and lies. In the end, we learned that Marcos had been taken by the OBAN.

* *Editor's note.* The Department of Social and Political Order was established in 1924 as the political police of São Paulo in charge of investigating, arresting, and interrogating people engaged in alleged subversive political activities. During the military regime, it became infamous as a site where officers tortured political prisoners. A *bandeirante* was a colonial backwoodsman who roamed the hinterlands of the state of São Paulo from the sixteenth century to the eighteenth, while Brazil was under Portuguese rule. Many were involved in capturing Indians to be sold into slavery. The *bandeirante* is the symbol of the state of São Paulo, although the negative images of this figure as a slave trader are rarely noted. Tiradentes Prison was the principle place in São Paulo where political prisoners were incarcerated.

The OBAN or Operation Bandeirantes was formed by the armed forces and financially supported by private businessmen. Its purpose was to "interrogate" individuals suspected of terrorist or subversive activities. A report published by Amnesty International in 1973 stated, "The *Operação Bandeirantes* is a type of advanced school of torture. It can be said that there are few people in São Paulo, and probably throughout Brazil, who have not read of *Operação Bandeirantes*, or OBAN or OB, in the Brazilian press."[*] Indeed, an article from the Brazilian magazine *Veja*, dated November 12, 1969, gave the following description:

> In São Paulo, the OBAN, an organization created by the Commander of the Second Army with the exclusive aim of arresting terrorists and subversive elements, has a relatively autonomous character. However, it received and continues to receive an extensive amount of information from the Secret Service of the Army, *Centro de Informações do Exército* (CIE) [Army Intelligence Center], and of the Navy, *Centro de Informações da Marinha* (CENIMAR) [Navy Intelligence Center], all located in Guanabara [state of Rio de Janeiro], the central headquarters for anti-terrorist activities. It recently changed its name to DOI (Departamento de Operações Internas do Exercito) [Department of Internal Operations of the Army].[†]

The OB was created in September 1969 by a group of 78 to 80 rightwing individuals from the Army, Navy, Air Force, and police force. Their aim was to create and equip a specialized police force to crush guerrilla groups and to "work over" any suspects.

[*] *Report on Allegations of Torture in Brazil* (Palo Alto, Calif.: Amnesty International, 1973), 18.
[†] "Estratégia para matar o terror," *Veja* (November 12, 1969): 27.

According to the journalist A. J. Langguth, who wrote about OBAN in his book *Hidden Terrors*:

Henning Albert Boilesen, the president of a liquid gas company, . . . had [originally] come to Brazil from Denmark as an official of the Firestone Rubber Company. Seventeen years later, he became a naturalized Brazilian citizen. He moved easily through São Paulo's prosperous society, picking up a host of influential friends: former minister Hélio Beltrão; Ernesto Geisel, the president of Petrobras; General Siseno Sarmento. He occupied a house on Rua Estados Unidos, and for years it was believed that this was not the only sense in which Boilesen lived on the United States.

The suspicion that Boilesen was a CIA agent grew when he began soliciting money for a new organization to be called Operação Bandeirantes (OBAN), in honor of the *bandeirantes*, the explorers and treasure hunters who had once trekked across Latin America. OBAN united the various military and police intelligence services in a crusade that went beyond normal jurisdictions.*

Amnesty International affirmed: "Torture is applied at the *Operação Bandeirantes* in a very precise manner, it does not vary and is routinely applied in a standardized fashion to all of the victims: torture plays an integral role within the system according to which the employees of the *Operação Bandeirantes* work, and this system is generally adhered to."[†]

The testimony of those tortured, however, speaks for itself.

THE "PARROT'S PERCH"

The parrot's perch consists of an iron bar wedged behind the victim's knees and to which his wrists are tied; the bar is then placed between two tables, causing the victim's body to hang some 20 or 30 centimeters from the ground. This method is hardly ever used by itself: its normal "complements" are electric shocks, the *palmatória* [a length of thick rubber attached to a wooden paddle], and [near] drowning . . . [Augusto César Salles Galvão, student, 21, Belo Horizonte, 1970.]

---

* A. J. Langguth, *Hidden Terrors* (New York: Pantheon, 1978), 122–23.
† Amnesty International, *Report on Allegations of Torture in Brazil*, 18.

... the parrot's perch was a collapsible metal structure ... which consisted of two triangles of galvanized tubing, of which one of the corners had two half-moons cut out, on which the victims were hung: the tubing was placed beneath their knees and between their hands, which were tied and brought up to their knees ... [José Milton Ferreira de Almeida, 31, engineer, Rio, 1976.]

ELECTRIC SHOCK

Electric shocks are given by an Army field telephone that has two long wires that are connected to the body, normally to the sexual organs, in addition to ears, teeth, tongue and fingers. [Augusto César Salles Galvão.]

The last resort is to try to get one prisoner to convince another to talk, as corroborated by a letter by Marlene de Sousa Soccas, a thirty-five-year-old dentist, written in 1972 to the judge of the military court in São Paulo:

Two months after my arrest, when I was in Tiradentes prison, I was brought back to OBAN again. My torturers believed that I was in contact with the geologist Marcos Pena Sattamini de Arruda, who had been tortured for the last month. I was carried into the torture room and one of the torturers, an army captain, said to me, "Get ready to see Frankenstein come in." I saw a man come into the room, walking slowly and hesitantly, leaning on a stick, one eyelid half closed, his mouth twisted, his stomach muscles twitching continuously, unable to form words. He had been hospitalized between life and death after traumatic experiences undergone during violent torture. They said to me, "Encourage him to talk, if not the 'Gestapo' will have no more patience and if one of you doesn't speak we will kill him and the responsibility for his death will lie with you." We did not speak, not because we were heroic, but simply because we had nothing to say.*

According to Article Fifty of the Universal Declaration of Human Rights, ratified by Brazil, "No one will be submitted to torture or cruel, humiliating treatment or punishment."

---

* Amnesty International, *Report on Allegations of Torture in Brazil*, 21.

It is difficult to describe what it was like during the twenty-four days that Marcos disappeared. My mother gives her own account in a letter dated May 9, 1970:

> The name of Octávio Medeiros, our friend and secretary to President Médici, opened doors for me. I was treated with the greatest courtesy and respect. My appearance as a grieving grandmother said everything. . . . Everywhere I went I spoke about the darkness we were living through and how Marcos had never been involved in "subversive" activities. I recounted his entire life story beginning when he was a little boy. I spoke about the fact that he had gone to Catholic schools, been in the Boy Scouts, received a scholarship to go to the United States, attended a Jesuit seminary, and received a degree in geology. I spoke about his marriage and his work in Petrópolis. Then I spoke about his divorce, which saddened us, because he had been very fond of his wife.

My mother tried to prove that Marcos was a kind and gentle person. The military only suggested that we go to the hospital to get more information about Marcos.

My mother, who was then seventy-five years old, suffered deeply over Marcos's situation and tirelessly tried to make contact with military officials at the highest levels, until, as she related in a letter, she was able to meet with the General who had sent us word of Marcos. Seeing her anguish, he sent a letter of introduction to the General Commander of the Second Army. Only in this way were we able to meet with the authorities, who could give us permission to visit the hospital where Marcos was confined.

My mother and Marcos's father repeatedly went to the Second Army hospital, but they were never allowed to see Marcos. By chance, during one of these visits they met a sympathetic nun, Sister Catarina, who was assigned to take care of my son. Through this Sister, they began to learn the truth about the state of his health.

They learned that Marcos was lying in the same hospital bed where Brother Tito, another victim of the military's brutal treatment of political prisoners, had been detained. Brother Tito was a Dominican friar who had been barbarously tortured and who had tried to commit suicide with the hope of calling the public's attention to what the military was doing. He knew the people would wonder why a priest would commit suicide. But it was all covered up, and the public didn't hear his story until much later. He had been tortured so badly that he was never the same. Later, when he was released from prison, he went to a monastery in France, where he hung himself in a tree in the garden.

It was through Sister Catarina that our family sent Marcos candy, pajamas, and letters, hoping that they would lift his spirits. Only the letters were delivered, though, and even then only after they had been censored.

Tearful and humble, my mother asked someone in the public relations office of the Military Hospital to tell Marcos that she and his father were there to help him and that they were doing everything possible to get him released.

We eventually discovered from other ex-prisoners that the OBAN had sent Marcos to the hospital on a stretcher and in desperate condition. They said his face was so deformed that he was recognizable only by his clothing.

The first word he was finally able to utter was "Padre" . . .

A chaplain, who was also a captain, was called to the hospital. He came to hear Marcos's confession but was accompanied by four police agents. The priest refused to hear Marcos's confession under such circumstances and insisted the police officers leave. Marcos used the privacy of the confession to recount how he had been tortured and nearly killed. He asked the priest to inform his family about where he was being held. The priest administered to Marcos his last rites and absolved him but did not do what Marcos had asked.

Later we learned that other political prisoners who had seen Marcos testified that he had been brutally tortured. When he couldn't take any more, his body had lapsed into violent convulsions. In addition, they said he had been forced to witness the torture of other prisoners, though Marcos never remembered this experience.

My mother and Marcos's father continued to go to the hospital daily, sometimes together and sometimes alone, but they were never allowed to enter or to see Marcos. Despite the fact that the law stipulated a prisoner could remain incommunicado for only ten days, they refused him any outside contact. The family would bring food and letters, which were delivered by Sister Catarina.

During one of my mother's visits to the hospital, she was told that if Marcos were pardoned and released, it would be wise for him to leave the country so that he might "be forgotten."

I still remained in the United States, where I lived and worked. I received many letters from my mother and children telling me that it wouldn't make any difference if I came to Brazil because I wouldn't be able to do anything more for Marcos. He still had to go before a judge before he could be released. He was now imprisoned in the hospital, where the beatings and torture continued, without the slightest notion of when or if he would ever see us again. Meanwhile, we had to live with our own fears and anxieties, the eternal "should I?" or "shouldn't I?" "will it be better?" or "will it be worse?" Only those who have experienced this—and they were many—can feel and comprehend what it means to be powerless for fear of doing something that will aggravate the situation.

Phone calls and letters from Rio sustained me during this period. Here are selections from some of them:

Letter from my daughter Mônica to me:

Rio, April 6, 1970

Things are going much better. I think that from here on out we won't have to worry as much. He's been found and can already receive visitors. [Unfortunately, this was not true—LPS]. Today Dad and Grandma are going to São Paulo to take care of things. So the first stage is over now, and we just have to be patient and work hard and wait for the rest, which could be six months or more . . .

We had a hard time while we were waiting for this news.

Grandma nearly lost hope. We had to insist that she not despair, that she had to be strong so that she could help him. We had to motivate her. In the beginning it was hard! She even threatened to commit suicide, can you imagine! But now she's much better and more calm.

Letter from my daughter Martinha to me:

Rio, June 8, 1970

I can well imagine how you're feeling at this moment. We are trying hard not to give in to the sorrow and pain. To the contrary, for each of us there is a lot of work ahead.

Sadly, it wouldn't do any good if you were to come here, leaving your work and everything. If there were really anything you could do, I would be the first to call you.

Letter from Martinha to me:

Rio, June 13, 1970

Today we received bad news: he's been hospitalized [again] with orders that he not be released. Nor may he be moved anywhere. Grandma goes there every day, but she hasn't been allowed to see him. The doctors say that he shouldn't be excited by having visitors. But we know this isn't the reason; they just don't want him to be seen by anyone.

They say that his status is one of slow recuperation, but we've received no diagnosis explaining exactly what it is he's recovering from.

With regard to your sending money, twenty or thirty dollars would help a lot to pay for the plane trips to São Paulo. I know you'll be upset with this news, but it's important to remember that this is better than nothing. Now we can act, we have concrete facts, we've received confirmation, etc.

Mom, I know it's hard, really hard, to endure this but don't despair, don't give up now. We're counting on your support. After all, you're the one who taught us to keep our chins up and to keep going . . .

Letter from Martinha to me:

Rio, June 23, 1970

I know you are probably despairing because distance and lack of fresh news only increases one's agony. Grandma told you everything we know: the state of his health, his improvements, the concern of the nun and the priest, the things the major slowly tells us, and even what the other workers at the hospital have said.

We received the $130.00 and got a great exchange rate. Thanks! It will be a great help.

Beyond this, for the time being, you shouldn't do anything more from there because you really might harm him here. You might close some of the doors that have opened for Grandma, who is on the verge of being able to see him.

Until now, Dad and Grandma have been treated very well there because we haven't gotten lawyers involved or anything. . . . When it's just the family, they open up more, you understand? They think there's less opposition, and so they're nicer. Who knows, maybe in the next little while we'll be allowed to see him?

It's obvious that everyone's worried—everyone's nerves are strung as tight as can be. That's why we think it's better for everyone to do everything possible to contribute to improving his situation, to his recovery, to providing information and influencing people . . . We have to try to lead a normal life, so we don't lose our nerves and health.

On one visit to the hospital, some of the doctors asked if Marcos were an epileptic or if he had been, because he was having convulsions that seemed like epileptic seizures. Despite their knowledge of the torture Marcos had endured, the military doctors were looking for evidence that Marcos's condition had not been caused by torture but was the result of hereditary problems.

We learned at this point that Marcos was trembling a lot and suffering from a neurological disorder affecting his motor skills. "They" also said he was being seen by psychiatrists, neurologists, and trauma specialists. [Later we discovered that this wasn't true.—LPS] We learned from others that his eyelids were drooping and that he could hardly walk. We also found out that he had been arrested and accused on charges of terrorism. To this day, nothing has been proven, except that he had been inspired by French and Belgian priests to get a job in a factory in order to help the other workers organize a union and give them spiritual support.

Only much later did we learn from Marcos himself that he had received electric shocks that had caused a neurological disorder that provoked convulsions. The doctors even requested that Marcos's father and I submit to an EKG to prove that Marcos had not inherited an epileptic condition.

In the hospital, the torturers returned daily to interrogate Marcos when Sister Catarina wasn't present. One weekend, two guards from the OBAN, who were in charge of overseeing Marcos, entered and began to hit his chest and stomach, while Marcos protected his face with his arms. Afterward, he was able to bend his legs only with great difficulty. He was trembling so much that he couldn't control them. Marcos was unable to cry out because the shocks previously given to his mouth had caused his tongue to swell. Only after some time and with great difficulty was his voice strong enough for him to ask for help.

Sister Catarina came in, and Marcos said, "Sister, sister, they're attacking me."

She turned to the guards and asked indignantly, "Did you do this?"

The guards responded by indicating with their fingers that he was crazy, "He's lost it, Sister."

Marcos asked to speak with the head of hospital security and begged him to stop the visits of the torturers. The security chief ordered that the guard be changed, and the two officers from the OBAN were replaced by soldiers from the Military Police. From then on, two soldiers stood guard outside his cell.

My mother and Marcos's father went to the hospital nearly every day in an attempt to see Marcos or at least find out more about his condition. Despite these visits and the countless messages they passed on to him, they were devastated to receive the following note from Sister Catarina: "On July 8, Marcos was taken back to the OBAN. He could walk only with the aid of a broomstick, since he was dragging his semi-paralyzed leg."

My mother and Marcos's father inquired why Marcos was being returned to the OBAN, but the only answer they received was that Marcos was fine and that he was only going back in order to write a deposition and to be brought face to face with Marlene, the woman with whom he had been arrested. A week later, he was returned to the hospital. They gave no explanation to my mother other than that he had had a "small relapse," due to the strain of writing and the emotional trauma of seeing Marlene. According to their version of events, Marcos had "fallen in love with her."

In a letter to Pope Paul VI, Marcos later explained what really happened to him during the week he was returned to the OBAN:

> I was sent back to OBAN, put in a cell, and told to write out a confession. . . . I finished this in three days, at the end of which time I was brought face to face with the woman whom I had been on my way to meet at the time of my arrest. It was six o'clock when I was carried into the room where she was kept. They wanted me to admit the name of the organization of which they believed I was a member, and they wanted me to give names of supposed comrades. They began to carry the woman into another room and gave her a strong electrical shock in order to make me talk (they were afraid to torture me again in view of my poor physical condition). I hear the cries of the girl being tortured;

and, when they brought her back into my room, she was shaking and totally distraught. I was paralyzed with fear at witnessing such cruelty and even more terrified when they threatened to do the same to members of my family if I didn't tell them what they wanted to know. They repeated the electric shock treatment on the girl and, seeing that they were not achieving anything, decided to call the doctor to examine me physically to see if I was fit to undergo more torture. The doctor ordered certain tablets and said that I should not be given food. They brought me back to my cell and were to return for me later. Having seen that they were ready to torture the woman again, and possibly members of my family as well, I decided to try to protect these people, and I agreed to write out another deposition.

It is absolutely astounding how they lied to my believing mother, who thought that Marcos was being protected by the officials with whom she spoke, even as he was once again being tortured and mistreated!

Mother wrote a letter from the hospital at this point:

From the hospital, I was once again sent to the OBAN, where I spoke with a "major" who received me very well and showed me Marcos's dossier. They know everything he has done: his work in the factory, his work with the church, even the mechanics course he wanted to take. The major said Marcos tried to swallow a paper with letters and numbers in code on it. This is what they want him to talk about, but he won't say anything. On Friday, the major gave me a piece of paper to write him a letter. I did, and he read and approved it. He then sent someone in to speak with him. Later, over the phone, he told me that Marcos had already "opened up" a little, revealing some information.

All lies! We later found out that Marcos never received such a letter, nor did he even know that his grandmother had been there.

In reality, Marcos only received a letter that had been doctored by his captors to include the following information: for now it's better not to hire a lawyer; you should only do so if you go to a hearing. There are specialized lawyers here, and one has already been recommended to us. They say that it's better not to have a lawyer so as not to make things worse.

During one of my mother's visits to the hospital following this second experience in the OBAN, she was able to observe several of the nurses and doctors who were treating Marcos. They appeared very anxious and uneasy, and my mother inquired so persistently as to why this was so that they finally admitted that Marcos's state of health was again extremely precarious. Much later, we learned from Marcos himself that at this time and for several days he had suffered a state of amnesia. From his cellmate he eventually discovered that he had been treated by a psychiatrist. After several examinations, the psychiatrist chose electroshock therapy as his treatment! Marcos received an initial charge, which left him unconscious for several hours. A few days later, he received a second charge. Slowly, he regained consciousness, but after this trauma he was weaker physically and psychologically than ever before.

When I heard from my mother that Marcos's state of health was "extremely precarious," I took the next plane to Rio.

From there, I went to São Paulo, where I hired a lawyer who instructed me as to what we should do. He insisted that it was of the greatest importance that we see Marcos. This was August 2, 1970, and Marcos had not been allowed to communicate with anyone outside of prison since he had been arrested in May.

The following day, terror-stricken yet resolved to fight if necessary, I went to the General Headquarters with my mother, who already knew several individuals there.

We were directed to the Public Relations Office, and I told the officer we met with that I had come specifically from the United States to see my son. After he consulted with his superiors, we were informed that I would be allowed to speak with the Commander of the Second Army. Our visit was as follows: My mother was not allowed to enter. He received me standing up. I was surrounded by other army officers.

I began speaking, "I am from the U.S. State Department. I have come to see my son for I have just learned that he is dying."

This startled the General, who asked in return, "He's dying? He's dying?"

"No," one of the officers said, "He's already gotten better."

The general cheered up and said, "Your son is hysterical. He's unable to see anyone in uniform without suffering convulsions."

I stood erect and said, "You would be too, if they had done to you what they have done to him."

The General didn't respond. Finally he said, "Well then, tomorrow you can see him at noon."

The conversation ended. I returned to the Public Relations Office, where my mother was waiting for me. I must have been livid because on my way back the public relations officer told me, "If you want to get something off your chest, ma'am, you can tell it to me. You can cry, swear, whatever you'd like, and it will be between you and me. But never tell your true feelings in front of the General."

I snapped back, "What I have to say I will say to you, sir, to the General, and even to the President, if I should have the chance. I am not afraid."

He didn't respond but made the following statement with a half-smile, "Ma'am, you and your mother should probably not eat before your visit tomorrow because you are going to see that he's 'a little different' now."

I left trembling with rage.

We arrived at the military hospital the following day at noon. The hour of truth had come. We were finally going to see Marcos after eighty-seven days of imprisonment. What we didn't know, though, was that the period of our greatest anguish was only about to begin.

Técio Lins e Silva, the lawyer I had hired, insisted that I bring a small camera with me, because a photograph of Marcos would be a piece of priceless evidence that could show the whole world what they had done to him.

Being inexperienced in this situation, however, I was terrified. I wasn't afraid of being hurt or getting arrested, but rather I feared that Marcos would disappear or that they would prohibit me from seeing him again, which would have been a big emotional blow to him. So I didn't bring the camera.

We were escorted by a young soldier who was a little drunk and who later confessed that he hated the army. He was visibly disturbed when I told him, after our visit, what they had done to Marcos. He said that he hadn't known about the torture and that he thought Marcos was just a sick soldier. He told us he would do everything he could to help. However, I never saw him again. Even worse, I could have photographed Marcos because the soldier didn't even stay in the cell with us!

My mother went in first. Marcos was unaware that I had returned to Brazil, and I didn't want to upset him with my sudden appearance. I made my mother promise not to react to how Marcos looked by crying, even though his appearance would upset her. We had to show only strength and love. She entered bravely and, after ten minutes, told Marcos that she had brought him a surprise. When I entered, the emotion we all felt was indescribable. We cried, laughed, and embraced until we were able to calm down enough to talk. The joy and horror that engulfed us couldn't be expressed without tears.

I smiled and said, "You're alive, you're alive, and that is all that matters."

He was shaking uncontrollably.

Marcos was physically changed. I later described his condition in a letter to the Minister of Justice in the Médici government, Alfredo Buzaid:

> Respected Minister, my son is an invalid!
>
> His left leg is paralyzed, and he can't move it. His right eyelid is almost shut, and the left is half-open. He suffers convulsions of the thorax, swallows only with great difficulty, and pronounces his "r"s doubled, as the French do.

I was worried that Marcos had suffered brain damage, and so I asked him in English, "Can you still speak English?"

He responded, "Yes, I can."

After verifying that his conversation was normal and rational, I asked him the question I feared, "Did they castrate you, my son?"

I had heard of cases in which young men suffered this as a result of being excessively beaten or tortured by electroshock.

"No," he said, "not that."

Then, he briefly told us everything that had happened to him. He complained especially about severe headaches and dizziness and told us that when the OBAN was on duty they would enter his cell and beat him severely.

Each time he mentioned being tortured, his body involuntarily and violently shook and his face grimaced.

Eventually our time was up, and we left his cell. We were crushed—incensed by the conditions in which we had found Marcos and terrified of the future.

I went to my cousin's house and immediately began writing a long letter to Alfredo Buzaid. My heart ached and my throat choked with disgust.

We had received permission to visit Marcos for a five-day period only. His brother, sisters, father, and grandmother visited him each day, though always only in groups of two. After visiting Marcos three times, I returned to Rio to meet with our courageous young lawyer, Técio Lins e Silva, to whom I am eternally indebted. Técio was fearless. He was one of the few lawyers willing to take on such a case as Marcos's. He never charged us a dime and wisely counseled us until we were able to safely leave Brazil.

We did everything possible to get Marcos released, but the wheels of "justice" were slow, if they moved at all. I went to the offices of the Minister of Justice and the Minister of the Army and gave them a report detailing everything that had happened to Marcos and emphasizing that no charges had been filed against him. I pleaded for his release on the grounds that it was impossible for him to defend himself. Nothing happened.

I was finally able to contact Manoel Ferreira Filho, the secretary to Justice Minister Buzaid and someone I already knew quite well, since he had been part of a group of visiting judges and lawyers I had accompanied and for whom I had interpreted for an entire month in the United States. I telephoned him in Brasília saying, "I need to see you. It's a matter of life and death."

He immediately responded, "It's about your son, isn't it?"

He was clearly already aware of what was going on.

We arranged a time to meet, and he came to Rio. We met in a closed room. There was a red light outside indicating that we shouldn't be disturbed.

He asked me, "What do you want me to do?"

"I want you to have my son transferred from São Paulo to Rio, and I want you to guarantee that they won't ever lay a hand on him again."

He banged the table with his fist and said, "I am against this business of torture, but I can't do anything."

I jumped up and said, "That is not true. You could denounce the practice of torture and leave this cruel government."

He silently lowered his head, and I continued, "I didn't come here to judge you but to ask for your help."

I explained to him the hardship of the family having to travel so frequently from Rio to São Paulo and of how my mother's efforts had exhausted her. I had to return to the United States, and I wanted our relatives to be near him. According to the doctors who had treated Marcos at the hospital, he needed to be taken care of at home by his family in order to get over his frequent convulsions and his terror.

Years later, when I was working as an interpreter alongside Marcos in

Mozambique with Paulo Freire and his team of educators, my son wrote a
poem in the silence of our hotel room:

> Grandmother, then
> Mother
> emerge through the door of my cell
> in the hospital.
>> It is the potency
>> of an uninterrupted chain
>> of life
>> in an unending spiral
>> from the first cell
>> down to me.
> It is the strength
> of our visceral bond
> pulsating
> there before us.
>> Humanity,
>> the plant growing greenest
>> in Nature's breast
> The protection of the maternal
> womb
> today has eternal
> worth
>> The old transforms itself into a great
>> fetus
>> and everything begins again.

I returned to Washington to my work, so that I could help cover the expenses we were incurring as a result of the many phone calls and trips we were making on Marcos's behalf. During this time, I continued to receive letters and news from my family. Marcos continued to be held by the military in São Paulo, and because I hadn't received an answer from Manoel Ferreira Filho, I decided to write him a long letter, which I sent to my daughter to deliver in person.

Here are some excerpts from that letter, which was dated August 15, 1970:

> Marcos is at an impasse. He cannot recover as long as he is prevented from leaving prison. He cannot leave prison until his case goes to trial. His case cannot go to trial until he recovers.
>
> The last time I was with him was on Wednesday. His condition worsened when they took his cellmate to be tortured again. Hugo Miguel Moreno is an Argentine, who is imprisoned without anyone in the world knowing because he had only been passing through Brazil when he was arrested. Hugo urinated blood, his legs were paralyzed, and his feet were cut from his being made to stand on open tin cans.
>
> Marcos felt so sorry for him he cried when the man was taken again to the OBAN, hardly able to walk. We fear for Marcos's life. His convulsions have gotten worse.
>
> I've learned that from the moment I returned to the United States, all visits were prohibited, and Marcos remains incommunicado, in accordance with the orders of the General Headquarters of the Second Army. You know very well that the law stipulates a maximum of ten days incommunicado, but three months have already gone by . . .

The only thing left for us is to wait for justice, which seems to me to become blinder with each passing day . . .

We are asking for legal representation as well as a legal medical examination to see if we can move him to a hospital we can trust where his family can be nearby. In the opinion of the military doctors, this is essential to his recovery. They say that it will take two years or longer for him to return to normal, if he can return at all.

I have to admit, though, that I was greatly disappointed to discover just how little influence your Minister, the Minister of War, and the other stuffed shirts that I met actually wield. After my visit to Brazil, I've come to the conclusion that our country is in the hands of a very small group, which is more powerful than even the president, and it's this group that controls the OBAN and those other horrible and illegal organizations and places.

All this talk about investigating reports of torture is purely to deceive the gullible, and, although you disagree among yourselves about these methods, you can't manage to get rid of them.

Marcos himself is a *corpus delicti*,* the perfect evidence for such an investigation, and from his own mouth I have learned that the most that can be done is to prevent him from being tortured again. Why won't you study his case? Why won't you visit him and see his wounds for yourself?

Dear friend, I've lost my faith in justice in Brazil. I will wait for my lawyer to contact me regarding our request for habeas corpus with representation, etc. If our request should be denied, there are still other avenues that I will pursue.

Three days later, I sent him the following telegram:

August 18, 1970 — Maneco, Great disappointment. Marcos worse again. Visits forbidden. General Headquarters never heard from you. Letter follows. Please take quick action. Lina.

I now tried to contact various international organizations, the principal one being Amnesty International, based in London. I tried contacting

* *Editor's note. Corpus delecti* is a Latin term used in Western jurisprudence to mean that one must prove that a crime has occurred before a person can be convicted for committing it.

everyone I knew within the U.S. labor movement, and I wrote letters to the Organization of American States (OAS), to the United Nations, and the International Commission of Jurists in Switzerland.

All of this now seems so surreal, as though it were out of a Kafka novel, but it is the truth. One need only see how worried the torturers became when they discovered that Marcos was not a worker, but came from a family with many connections and friends and had a mother working in the United States for USAID, a division of the State Department.

There must not have been good communication within the military, since those at the top, as I've said many times, did not control those beneath them. This will later become much more obvious, but just as an example: in São Paulo, during one of our three visits to Marcos, the hospital director spoke with my mother and me in private, "Tell him to talk. Tell him and insist if you must, so that 'they' will stop coming here and hurting him . . ."

While I was still in São Paulo, my mother and I were once again asked to voluntarily submit to an EKG in order to confirm that the convulsions Marcos was suffering were "caused by a hereditary defect and not because of the tortures." Marcos's father was asked to do the same in Rio.

So I went in to the very hospital where Marcos was being held to submit to the procedure.

We, my mother and I, were taken to a small room where we met a nurse who administered the electrical scan. When he was finished, he closely examined the results and said, "Just as we thought, Ma'am, you too are an epileptic, and you are going to suffer an attack within the next fifteen minutes."

I was confused for a second, but I quickly "woke up" and said, "Mom, we're getting out of here because this is a circus, and I am not a clown."

The man didn't say anything, and we left.

As I mentioned earlier, we later learned that Marcos suffered a profound spell of amnesia after spending the second week at the OBAN. They had called in a psychiatrist, and Marcos was treated with electroshocks.

We tried to counter their diagnosis by collecting statements from his friends, as well as the priests who had been his teachers in high school. They all said that Marcos had always attended class in perfect health and that he had never suffered a single convulsion. These testimonies were ignored by the military, and the terrors continued.

After I returned to the United States, my mother wrote me a series of letters, quoted below, updating me on what she could learn about Marcos's condition.

Rio, August 17, 1970

As we had planned, Mildo [my ex-husband—LPS] and Mônica remained in São Paulo until Friday night, and they were able to see Marcos on Thursday and on Friday, though only after many, many requests. He was relatively well, but he's had small convulsive relapses every day.

They placed another young man in the room with Marcos, and an agent came to interrogate him, which made Marcos very upset. The young man was transferred, though, and Marcos is by himself again. We speak with the Sister every day.

The letters continued to come, and I continued to cry and pray for better news. I couldn't sleep, and I don't know how I kept working.

Letter from my mother to Marcos:

Rio, August, 18, 1970.
My dear little Marcos,

I was there this morning to see you, but it wasn't possible. I am trying again to receive permission. I hope that you are feeling better and that your convulsions have stopped.

Letter from my mother to me:

Rio, September 2, 1970

I have tried to write every other day to keep you updated on every-thing. The director of the hospital says that Marcos is constantly im-proving, but tomorrow the neurologist who has been treating Marcos is going to give us an update.

Elza [my sister and Marcos's aunt—LPS] went up to the Laran-jeiras Palace to speak directly with Colonel Medeiros [Octávio Medeiros, secretary to President Médici and the husband of Elza's sister-in-law—ed.]. He explained everything that had been presented against Marcos and told her that even though Marcos has not been linked to violence, bank robberies, bombs, etc., what he was doing is also considered to be subversive. But his case isn't grave. The Colonel promised he would continue to keep an eye on him and that we might expect a solution sooner than we had thought.

When I received this news, I couldn't help but ask myself, who is it that's in control in that country? If all of these steps allegedly are being taken by the secretary to the President, why can't they take Marcos to a private hospital while he's waiting to be judged and released? The letter continued:

With regard to the Supreme Military Court, his case has still not been heard by them, and this is one of the reasons they won't let us see him.

In reality, the military was not preparing a case against Marcos.* His name was only included in a military case three months after he was released and one year after he had been arrested.

While all of this took place, I was suffering far away, in the United States, worrying about Marcos, as well as about my other children, who lived under the threat that they too might be "interrogated."

I continued working, however, because we needed all the money we could get to pay the phone bills (which were more than $200 a month!) and for the airfare to São Paulo. We constantly sent letters and notes to encourage him, but we couldn't hide our interminable fear that Marcos would meet the same fate as so many others who had disappeared or had been murdered. Though it was a relief at least to know where Marcos was, the terror continued, and with good reason, because he was in the power of the OBAN.

In my loneliness and pain, crying and praying, I wrote him the following letter:

Oh, my son!

How everything reminds me of the past! "I made a wish and you came true." Oh, the joy of a firstborn son! The sensation that one is a mother and is holding her own little being who is living and breathing.

I was so young myself, and I was so emotional when the doctor told me I was pregnant.

* *Editor's note.* This was likely the case because the authorities had not collected any evidence to prove that Marcos had violated the National Security Act or any other law.

I went home and laughed by myself all day long. My God, I'm going to have a son! What a beautiful thing! Oh, Marcos, it is so difficult to put into words all of the moments, all of the hours full of love, dedication, and devotion that a mother feels for each child. This love grows and grows and expands until there's no space left. It never ends! It never changes!

In a mother's mind, a child never grows up! He always remains the baby you nursed and whose diapers you changed.

A child represents our own hope of seeing accomplished everything that we were never able to do.

A child is a piece of his mother's heart and soul, and when he goes out into the world, he always carries his mother's joy, pride, hope, and an infinite dose of sweetness and concern.

To you, my beloved son, I dedicate my heart, with endless love, goodness, patience, and gentleness.

Your hopeful mother.

These and other letters from the entire family and the responses that we received from him thirty days later kept Marcos alive while he remained in solitary confinement and under constant fear that he might be tortured again.

Letter from my mother to me, August 12, 1970:

I've fought to see Marcos here in São Paulo for the last three days. Dr. Aquino, Marcos's doctor in the hospital, told me yesterday that Marcos's spirits are very good, though his neurological system was still improving slowly. He asked me to go the General Headquarters and ask for permission, in his name, as Marcos's doctor, to see Marcos.

I went there immediately, and, after I waited a long time, they informed me that the doctors have to make an official request of this kind in person. So the afternoon was gone, and I had accomplished nothing.

Elza spoke with Medeiros, who spoke told General Albuquerque that I wanted to see the General. I went and had to wait for a long time, because he was in a meeting. Finally, though, I was received very well. I explained everything to him about Marcos's improvement. He sent me to speak with General Coutinho, who determined that I should speak with General Canavarro, the highest officer of the Second Army. I had already written a letter to General Canavarro, asking for permission to see Marcos on advice of his doctors. It was a long and beautiful letter, appealing to his feelings as a grandfather and to his sense of justice. I was received in a room by a pleasant colonel who took my letter to the General. I learned, however, that he is a myth; he doesn't meet with anyone.

After a long time, the colonel returned and told me that he wouldn't be able to grant me permission to visit Marcos, for we had already received an exception when you were here with me. To my great surprise, though, he said that Marcos would be transferred to the Army Hospital in Rio and that, as soon as he improved, his case would be heard there.

I don't know who made this possible, but I overheard the colonel, talking on the telephone, mention the name General Adalberto Pereira dos Santos, who represents the Supreme Court of Rio. I left devastated because I hadn't received permission to see him, but since it was still early, I went to the hospital to drop some things off for Marcos. I arrived, but there was no one there. The directors had all left, so the doorman, who I knew very well by this time, took me inside to find the official on duty, Lieutenant Amado. I don't know if it was because he saw how sad my face was, but he offered to let me see Marcos for five minutes . . .

He was sleeping peacefully and had good color. When I called to him he looked radiant—he had been sorely disappointed that I had not been to see him. I quickly told him of my earlier meeting and then I gave him the news that he was going to be transferred to Rio, which cheered him up significantly.

I noticed he still trembled, and his eyes were still the same. The convulsions are getting better. As long as he is kept there, he will not improve because of his nervousness and insecurity.

I could almost die to see him. He looks like the very worst of criminals. He's been isolated for nearly four months, and he's sick. Yet, they think they've done such a great thing to let us see him for five days.

Chapter Six

After discovering that Marcos would be sent to Rio, my younger son Miguel wrote the following undated letter to him:

You can't imagine our happiness to discover that you are coming to Rio. We are thrilled and feel much closer to you. Be cool, my brother, and I'll see you soon. I'll always be down at the door delivering things to you until I can see you again.

Letter from my mother:

Rio, August 24, 1970

I'm now writing from Rio, since Marcos has been transferred here. It happened because of the request made by Medeiros, who made a recommendation to some high officials within the Ministry of War.

It was General Canavarro's personal secretary who told me when I was in São Paulo that Marcos would be sent here.

The day after I was told, I went to the hospital with Martinha, and the good Lieutenant Constantino gave us the news that an order had been received requesting Marcos be transferred to Rio. Everyone at the hospital was very bewildered by the news, and the lieutenant asked us to pretend we didn't know what was going on as long as we were around the directors. Even so, he let us visit with Marcos for 20 minutes.

Last Friday, I tried to see him in São Paulo before he was transferred to Rio, but I wasn't allowed to because they were installing some machines. I arrived home around eleven and the lieutenant telephoned to tell me that they were preparing Marcos for the trip to the Military Hospital in Rio. The lieutenant said that the Sister was packing his bag and that an ambulance was waiting along with two excellent nurses, who are our friends.

That afternoon, I returned to the hospital. I bought some boxes of chocolates to offer to the directors, to thank them and say goodbye.

The two directors were there together, and they received me very well. As the lieutenant had advised, I asked how Marcos was. Both of them said, without blinking an eye, that he was feeling a little better, but they didn't say a word about his being moved to Rio.

I told them that I had been to the General Headquarters and visited with Colonel Agostini, who had told me that at any moment Marcos would be going to Rio. They both feigned astonishment but didn't do anything.

I became very upset and left without giving the chocolates to anyone.

I left immediately for Rio. The others in Rio have been to the hospital several times already, but they've been told he's not there. Major Sadi telephoned me yesterday, just before I left for Rio, confirming that Marcos was taken to the Central Hospital of the Army in Rio accompanied by two individuals of the utmost integrity. He said that the order came from Rio, but that they don't want to admit it, perhaps because his paperwork hasn't arrived there yet.

I'm going to go there today with a letter from a colonel of the National Intelligence Service, who works with Maria Helena Vidal. I am also going to go with [my sister—LPS] Elza to the General Headquarters to speak with another colonel recommended by Medeiros.

As for Maneco, the secretary to Buzaid, Sadi said that, as of Friday, they had still not received any instructions from him in São Paulo regarding Marcos.

Letter from my mother to me:

Rio, August 25, 1970

Yesterday Elza and I began our pilgrimage once again. First we went to the Minister of War, where we accomplished nothing. Everyone's in Brasília for Veterans' Day. From there we went to the hospital. As always, their ill will is clearly evident. We waited at the entrance while I called Maria Helena's friend, the colonel, who had taught me to ask, "Was so-and-so transferred from active duty to the hospital?" The men at the front desk looked in all their books but were unable to find any records. So I was sent to speak with the Military Police over at the Barão de Mesquita Headquarters. We went, and they were very polite. While I was explaining to one of the guards what it was that we wanted, a young man in civilian clothes approached us and asked, "Ma'am, are you trying to find out about an "epileptic" young man who arrived from São Paulo to undergo specialized treatment?"

I said yes, and he left to check into it. He returned and said that Marcos was in the hospital but was not allowed to receive visitors, phone calls, or any other form of communication. He was being monitored by the civilian police, but his case was under the authority of the Military Police.

Now read Marcos's own description of what really happened when he arrived in Rio:

You asked what happened when they brought me to Rio? I believe it was in August 1970. I came in an ambulance that was tightly locked up. The torturers were armed and sat in the front. I was only removed when we arrived in the inner courtyard of the Military Police at the Barão de Mesquita Headquarters. They forced me to take off my clothes, except for my socks, in order to search me. The entire time I was there, I had to wear a black hood. After a long while, maybe two hours, I was taken to the Military Hospital.

The doctor who examined me was Dr. Boia, which was an appropriate name for such a corpulent man. He was also the captain responsible for security at the Military Hospital. I remember the patio was very agreeable, with some trees and cool shade, and I can also remember the entrance to the hospital ward where I was taken. They made me change into some pajamas and then they locked me in a room with bars on the window. I remained there, lying in the bed for three weeks, completely alone. The man who brought my food wouldn't say two words to me. The doctor assisted the torturers. He was the one who supervised the condition of political prisoners and released them when he thought they were healthy enough to be tortured again. During these first weeks, the nurses also didn't communicate with me. Because of this and also because of the lack of contact with my family, my primary memory is that of virtually complete loneliness. I was once again incommunicado, but I though that my situation had improved because I was far away from the torturers of the OBAN and closer to my family.

It was only later that I was transferred to a large prison infirmary with several beds and one or two other political prisoners who were there temporarily. Several regular prisoners were also there, like the boy with a broken femur, who had been nearly murdered by the civilian police while trying to steal a car. Even before they had identified whether he was a common criminal or a political prisoner, the military repression nearly killed him.

Mother's account continues:

We have nearly half of the world interested in his case. We asked the local chaplain to administer communion to him. Tomorrow it seems that the Supreme Court will rule on his habeas corpus. Now we just have to get them to deliver the fruits and sweets to Marcos as we were doing in São Paulo.

The doctor from the Neurological and Psychiatric division is a good friend of Nair's and Lia's [Marcos's cousins—ed.], and they say he is a good man.

Things are beginning to fall into place. Just knowing that he won't be returning to the OBAN must be a great relief to Marcos.

Letter from my mother to my daughter Tiana:

Rio, August 27, 1970

I've just arrived home from the Military Hospital where Marcos was transferred.

Yesterday, Elza was able to speak on the phone with the captain of security, who was very polite and who confirmed that Marcos had arrived and had already been seen by a doctor. He said that in the prison infirmary there is always a doctor and two nurses on duty. He also said that what Marcos needs now is plenty of exercise to move his leg so that it doesn't atrophy. He has permitted us to bring gifts and letters for Marcos.

As for visits, it is out of his hands, though he thinks they would only do him good. He gave me the name of a major in the Ministry of War who could give me a card to take to the Military Police that would permit visits twice a month, on Thursdays.

I am not feeling very well, without energy to do anything. I stayed at home crying and praying while Elza went to take care of this. She has been tireless, willing, and unembarrassed, while at each step I am timid and everything has required great effort. I work like an ant, tamely digging through each new barrier. Your brothers and sisters disagree with me. They want aggression, and I would probably be in jail already if I listened to them.

Letter from my mother to me:

Rio, August 29, 1970

We were not allowed to see Marcos today because all of his paperwork from São Paulo hasn't arrived. It seems that we won't be able to visit him until the 8th and then only two at a time, according to the officer of the CODI, who has given us permission for this.

There are no serious charges against him, and he is very well protected by the recommendations from São Paulo and from those by Medeiros here.

Elza has been tireless. I can already write to Marcos saying that I have continued my work on his behalf and that he can trust in me. I hope that, when you return in October, things will already be much clearer and everything will have ended.

Today Martinha went to deliver your letter to Maneco. She said that he was listless and declared that they had told him that they weren't allowing the family to see him because he was still in a bad state and having ongoing convulsions. But that's a lie because, as I already wrote to you, I saw Marcos in São Paulo just before he was transferred, and he was in good health and seemed very calm.

This confirmed my suspicions that it had not been on account of Maneco, my contact in the Ministry of Justice, that Marcos was transferred to Rio because he didn't even know what was really going on.

Letter from my mother to me:

Rio, August 31, 1970

Marcos's health is much better here in Rio. Elza, with all of her dedication went to Laranjeiras Palace and spoke with Medeiros. She had to wait for a long time because of all the activity surrounding the arrival of President Médici. She went without telling me so that I wouldn't be concerned.

Medeiros told her that since her first request he began to take an interest in Marcos's situation and that he had called São Paulo and recommended that the greatest care be taken with him. He also sought out all of the details of his legal case. He said that Marcos has been indicted as a member of Ação Popular and because of his work to raise consciousness among factory workers. Though this activity is considered less serious, it is still thought to be dangerous [by the military government] because it could "subvert the masses little by little." He said that he has done everything in his power to help Marcos's situation, telling them that Marcos came from an excellent background, had had an excellent education, and had been traumatized by several family matters, including his separation from his wife . . .

It was Medeiros, though, who was able to arrange for Marcos's transfer to Rio, since the hospital here has specialized treatments, and he even spent an entire day in São Paulo, when Marcos was still there, seeing to the details and necessary orders.

Letter from Miguel to me:

Rio, August 31, 1970

The first few days after you left were very disappointing. It seemed like the beginning all over again. All news was cut off, and they started all over with their charade of "he's doing well," etc.

We spent four days in a row visiting the hospital here in Rio, but nothing came of it! We were terrified that something had happened. On the fifth day, we learned that he had in fact arrived on the first day we visited and that for "bureaucratic" reasons he hadn't "officially" arrived. As for visits? They were prohibited!

As for the legal proceedings, we learned that the habeas corpus issue was about to be ruled on and that he had already spoken with several of the judges. We also learned that it has been proven that he is not in any way guilty and that he is being considered innocent by the military.

Letter from my mother to me:

Rio, September 5, 1970

Marcos is continually improving, according to the Captain who has been assisting us. The Captain is a good man and wonderful; all he needs to do is kiss me and call me grandma.

He gives us detailed reports on Marcos's condition, and I can write Marcos letters and even send goodies and games. Next week we are going to see him, and so that is really the good news that I have. I am tired. I've always done everything I could for you, and I've given all that I have right now. It's because of the great love that I have for you all that has led me to do this, not because of my own virtue. I expected at any moment, after Marcos was taken, to die of pain, knowing how much he had suffered, but I couldn't run away, I had to act. Everyone began working and an old lady with white hair, a grandmother crying for her grandson always has a strong effect.

I spent many nights in mourning, there in São Paulo, and suffered alone in my pain.

Now another good word has been sent on Marcos's behalf by General Muricy to General Siseno Sarmento, the commander of the First Army.

I have faith now that everything will be resolved more quickly than we had hoped and that soon we will take care of him and he will be okay.

Letter from my mother to Marcos, written after their first visit since Marcos had been in Rio. He arrived in Rio on August 26, 1970:

Rio, December 9, 1970
Dearest Marcos:

Our visit was such a joy, a ray of light in our lives. The only shadow was not seeing you in a perfect state of health.

Only my faith in Jesus and Mary has enabled me to survive the terrible ordeal we are going through.

I hope you are able to exercise your leg well, even in bed, and that next time you will be able to look at me with your eyes wide open.

Letter from Miguel to Marcos:

Rio, September 13, 1970
My Dear Brother:

We were so happy to be able to visit you! I hope I can go next time. I'm going with Dad and Mônica on 9/24. Mom calls all the time and sends a million kisses to you. She's coming back in October, remember? Just a little while longer!

Letter from Martinha to Marcos:

Rio, September 24, 1970

We want to see you again, may God grant that it's soon. Is your leg getting better with the exercises? Trust in us, we are always thinking about you. Grandma is very depressed and her health has gone downhill. We're very concerned for her. As long as she doesn't find you well, I don't think she'll get better. Every day she seems weaker, but we are taking good care of her.

Letter from Miguel to Marcos:

Rio, September 27, 1970
My Dear Brother:

We are anxiously looking forward to next week to be able to visit you again. Our separation has been very hard. Your friends are always asking about you. They all miss you and want to see you.

Every Sunday morning I'm here at the entrance of the hospital just to be near you.

Lucinha [Miguel's wife — LPS], Dad, Mônica, we're all with you at least in spirit . . .

Letter from Martinha to me:

Rio, September 24, 1970

Today was the day scheduled for our visit to Marcos. They wouldn't allow it. They wouldn't say why, and now we have to wait until next week. Things (except for the annoyance of not being able to visit him) are improving slowly.

We received a letter from Marcos. His handwriting is very bad, but at least it's his . . . There's still no word on visiting, though.

Our lawyer, Técio, said that next week there should be a ruling on his legal representation (though not on habeas corpus), and from there any result could come, including the best of all. We are going to be there for the ruling! Técio will be defending him. Thanks for the $300.

Some letters from Marcos

Letter from Marcos to his grandmother:

July 1970

My health is improving. "The light shineth in darkness; and the darkness comprehended it not." I am trying to reproduce within myself a little of the life of Christ.

I might be moved from here soon, but keep trying to see me.

Grandma and Dad, I don't know how to thank you for everything you have done for me. My sister has also been an angel. I cried a lot over Mom's beautiful letter and the confidence she has in me. May God grant that everything be resolved and that I am released soon.

Letter from Marcos to me:

Rio, September 17, 1970
Mommy Dearest:

I'm writing from the hospital, but I'm now in Rio. Your heart was right as always. Soon after you wrote me, "The claw that tightened is now loosening." I was permitted to have visitors again: Grandma and Martinha. Can you imagine my joy?

I applied all of my strength of will to the treatments. I have tried to be patient and courageous. But I wish you were closer to me, with your mother's intuition, which has been unfailing. The hours go by slowly. My recovery is slow-going, they say, and the future is cloudy.

The one certainty I have is that my suffering is not in vain. Elisabeth Lesieur wrote: "When a soul lifts itself up, an entire world is lifted as well." I pray especially for peace in the world.

Letter from Marcos to my mother:

Rio, September 18, 1970

How hard it is to wait for the time to go by! I am very anxious for the day of your visit to arrive. When you come, that half hour simply disappears. Oh, how I miss you so much! Who knows, but maybe you'll be able to see me more often?!! I constantly pray that my innocence will be recognized.

Letter from Marcos to the family:

Rio, September 21, 1970

Fifteen days go by so slowly! It seems like a century since I saw Grandma and Martinha. My dear Miguel, you were so close to me yesterday, but we weren't allowed to see each other. Do everything you can so that we can see each other more often. When you visited me in São Paulo, I was so dumbfounded and unable to say or ask anything. May God grant that everything go well, as you said, and that you will soon have me with you again. Dear Miguel, keep writing your touching and friendly letters that give me such strength and hope. Every day I exercise in the gym. The therapists think I am improving, though my health on the whole will require some time to return to normal.

Dear Grandma, Tiana is right in saying that you are the best Grandma in the world. I dream of leaving here soon and beginning to repay you, as little as it might be, for you deserve the world for what you have done for us and especially for me.

And what about Mom, Grandma? I would like her to be back here so I can see her, and hug her and have her strength near to me.

Letter from Marcos to my mother:

Rio, September 27, 1970

It was sad not to be able to see you last Thursday. Do everything you can to come soon. I miss you so much and pray that these difficulties will soon pass.

Letter from my mother to me:

October 2, 1970

Since September 10, when Martinha and I last saw Marcos, we have not been allowed to see him. After crying and begging over the phone, I went over on Thursday. Captain Morais said that he had a surprise for me, that "the boy was going to leave," but they decided they needed to wait a little longer.

It's because of the treatments, massages, and physical exercise for his leg. He's already beginning to walk in the infirmary, supporting himself on the beds. He has also improved mentally; he's wanted to improve ever since he found out that he wouldn't be going back to São Paulo. They told me that I'm not the only one fighting for Marcos, but that there are a lot of "good" people doing the same.

We later learned that they would not allow him to leave as long as there was any sign that he had been tortured. But they were defeated as long as they couldn't pass as the truth a lie that Marcos's condition was the result of being an epileptic.

Letter from Marcos to Miguel:

October 10, 1970

It is ten o'clock Sunday morning, and I'm silently concentrating and praying that you will be given permission to visit me. Far away I hear the strains of classical music. My only desire is to be with you and I know how much you are suffering for me. But after the storm comes the calm. . . . The challenge is to have the patience of Job, the courage of David and the love of Jesus. . . .

I've been playing my flute and fife and I feel you all so close; my heart is like a volcano ready to explode.

Noon: I've just received your letters. You know, I already loved you all so much, but absence and the impossibility of seeing you has infinitely increased my love. . . . It will be so good when I am there with you again! May God grant it happen soon! You all know how I've always tried to live according to the teachings of Jesus, who sustains me in every moment.

Letter from my mother to Marcos:

Rio, October 14, 1970

Everything in this world is fleeting; only God is eternal. Your suffering and detention will also pass away, and we will yet be reunited in our old family conversations, especially when your mother returns, sooner or later.

Letter from Marcos's father to Marcos:

Rio, October 15, 1970
Dear Marcos, May God bless you!

Yesterday the Supreme Military Court voted to end the ban on communication with you! We will see it happen any day now, how wonderful!

Today I hope to have the pleasure of personally meeting Captain Morais, a man of such humanity and understanding that from the first moment he won over our entire family. A thousand kisses and hugs to you my dear son. Tchau!

Letter from Marcos to his father:

Rio, October 16, 1970

What excellent news your letter brought me! Now I am more anxious than ever to see you all. When, when will it be? When I read your note, I gave a shout for joy! And I showed it to everyone here. May God grant that this becomes a reality! I have been well treated here. I miss you all very much. May God give me the chance to thank you all for everything you have been to me.

Letter from Marcos to his grandmother:

Rio, October 16, 1970

Yes, yes, we will soon see each other, I am sure of it. I am so anxious to see you again, Grandma! Now, the most important step has been achieved in the Supreme Military Court. I pray for you every moment, with patience, yet burning with anxiety. When will Mom return? That's when the party will begin. I hope you feel more at peace now. God is great! You have been so much for me in every way that He had to intervene!

As the family comforted Marcos in Rio de Janeiro, I worked in Washington, D.C., to obtain my permanent residency, in case we needed to get Marcos out of the country.

Letter from me to Marcos:

Washington, D.C., October 22, 1970

When I arrived in Washington, I received two of your letters the same day. They were a balm and an inspiration. Your courage, patience, and strength of spirit make me so proud, and they give me the courage to fight. I read a thought in a magazine that says: "No one understands that you have already given EVERYTHING. You must give more . . ." I think that this applies to the two of us, right?

I'm sorry that I can't give you the date when I will be able to return, but I should wait until my paperwork is all ready. It's important for us. Only God knows the sacrifice that it is for me to stay here, without being able to get on the plane now and go to you. But . . . "you must give more" . . .

Yesterday, I had a long conversation with Bill Doherty and Jessie, a friend of John's, who are going to do everything possible to facilitate my paperwork. In the meantime I'll have to wait.

But your letters are my joy in life!

Your handwriting has improved so much! You can already write so clearly and legibly! Was it very hard? Can you tell me more about your treatment? I would like to know everything!

I promise to write always, without stopping. I pray that my business here goes quickly so that I can return by November 15. How does that sound?

Your inconsolable Mom.

Letter from Marcos to my mother:

Rio, October 25, 1970

You can be certain that I feel in me the effect of all the love that each of you have shown me. And, especially, on Thursdays and Sundays, I concentrate harder and try "to send" my love to you all.

Letter from Marcos to my mother:

Rio, October 27, 1970

It's eight o'clock at night. These have been difficult days for me, and in my solitude and silence, I have placed my trust in the Lord with greater force and hope.

Letter from Marcos to my mother:

Rio, October 28, 1970

I received the letters. So, I'm going to have a little radio? The painting materials never came. But I am anxious to see you and give each one of you a long hug. Oh God, patience! In reality, I don't understand why things are taking so long. I'm doing everything I can to get better as soon as I can, and I push myself with my leg, though it hurts. Oh, the pain of being separated! When is Mom coming? Oh may you all come soon, please!

During this exchange of letters, I spoke with my family nearly every day by phone. In order not to go crazy, I worked almost nonstop. Joe DeFonzo, our contractor at the Agency for International Development, was a great friend. He also tried to assign me to trips with small groups so that I could get paid time and a half. These trips were very difficult for me, since I was not allowed to talk about my situation with visitors from Brazil. I had to smile and be good humored, even as I suffered deeply inside.

I wrote letters to all of the recommended agencies that might have been able to help. I still clearly remember the responses I received from the Organization of American States (OAS) and the United Nations. They went something like this: We are very sorry, but we are not permitted to interfere in the internal affairs of a country. I was shocked! "Then why do you exist?" I thought.

I worked for the OAS for almost twenty-five years as a freelance interpreter, and I am proud that I worked at meetings of the Inter-American Commission on Human Rights. The meetings were heated, and representatives from the countries accused of not adhering to the changes in its charter — namely the military dictatorships of Latin America, including Brazil — were quite annoyed at criticism leveled against them.

At one General Assembly meeting, a South American country refused to sign the final report because it had been accused of human rights violations. We stayed up until four in the morning, when an agreement was finally reached regarding a change of a single word in a sentence, and the ambassador signed.

The world had finally awakened to the truth about what was happening in so many countries in the Americas. Until then, the press had played a crucial role in revealing the atrocities being committed and the dangers of a spreading Nazi-like fascism in these countries. Before this, there was no official recognition of such gross violation of human rights.

In Rio, Marcos's situation remained the same, despite the promises and declarations, and even victory in the Supreme Military Court. For Marcos and for us it was like a drill slowly boring into an open wound, ever widening, purposely and with great pain, and without any pity.

Fortunately, the letters continued. We kept hoping for permission to visit, and the family kept vigil at the door of the hospital. I remained in the United States trying to resolve other related problems, but we all lived the same life, with the same hope: the release of Marcos from the hospital and our all being reunited again!

Letter from my mother to me:

Rio, October 7, 1970

He's read a lot, since we've sent many books on art, science, and poetry. Every Thursday and Sunday I send him some homemade food for lunch, besides the treats. As for me, I'm not sick at all, though I have suffered and continue to suffer!

Letter from Martinha to Marcos:

Rio, October 8, 1970

We are trying everything! I have faith that we will succeed. Your letter was marvelous; it was just like you! No one gets tired of reading and rereading and rereading it.

Grandma is trying to console herself, but she's still very anxious and low.

Miguel doesn't know what to do to calm himself; he's so anxious to see you after such a prolonged and difficult wait.

Are you able to open your eyes any wider? Can you see well? How are you in general? Dear Marcos, have faith, we are going to see each other soon, and Grandma really needs to see you. She is only living for this!

Letter from Marcos to my mother:

Rio, October 8, 1970

The minutes and hours drag on as long as I am away from you. The more I read and exercise, the more my thoughts are with all of you. Yesterday, I spent the morning concentrating on my hope that you all would appear here by my side.

My eye has improved a lot, and my leg is getting stronger.

Yes, I too need to see you, and I have faith in God that this will happen soon. May God take good care of my grandmother. And Mom comes on the 30th?

Letter from Miguel to Marcos:

Rio, October 11, 1970

Unfortunately, my dear brother, here we are once again being refused entry.

Letter from my mother to Tiana:

Rio, October 11, 1970

The writ of habeas corpus [in Brazil] has been suspended since December 1968, but, nevertheless, our appeal will be heard on Wednesday. Depending on the decision, your case will move on to civil court. We have received guarantees that they could also issue an order to free you.

Letter from my mother to me:

Rio, October 15, 1970

In the Supreme Military Court, the lawyer made an excellent presentation, but the prosecutor, in his accusation, made the biggest gaffe, saying that Marcos was seriously involved in the Operation Bandeirantes, which is a highly subversive organization. He didn't even know what the O.B. was. . . . It was such a scene, I nearly cried out in shock. I even think this helped Marcos's case.

Today, I, Lina, say, Yes, Operation Bandeirantes was a highly subversive organization against human rights, against decency, against justice, against dignity, against humanity. It was one of Brazil's greatest disgraces and is comparable only to the barbarities committed by the Nazis in the Holocaust.

In order to alleviate our anguish, we continued to exchange letters — sweet letters, filled with both enthusiasm and desperation.

Chapter Eight

Letter from my mother to me:

Rio, no date

. . . during the hearing the prosecutor said that Marcos had been indicted for being subversive, but the defense rebutted the entire story, mentioning your letter to Buzaid, and told about the bad treatment Marcos had received. He said that you, Lina, had hired a lawyer and that you were under contract with the State Department. In short, everything went well. Then came the pitiful little prosecutor, who could hardly read well and finished that horrible gaffe about the OBAN. Afterward, Marcos's lawyer Técio spoke. He spoke well, with a clear and strong voice, without any flourishes or bombastic phrases.

We then left, and the rest of the session was conducted behind closed doors. Fifteen minutes later we were allowed to reenter, and the president of the court read aloud that, by a unanimous vote, Marcos would no longer be held incommunicado!

Letter from my mother to Marcos:

Rio, October 23, 1970

I learned from the captain that the doctor has ordered you to stop reading so much, and I think you should do what he says. Don't force your brain with too many complicated things.

Letter from Miguel to Marcos:

Rio, October 25, 1970

Another week has gone by, and we haven't been allowed to see you. It's so hard! I don't understand why it's taking so long. The Supreme Military Court declared that you are no longer incommunicado. After everything that our family has gone through, it now seems that we are now fighting and suffering for no reason at all.

Letter from my mother to me:

Rio, October 28, 1970

I am already an old woman, and I keep up my spirits only because of the love I have for my grandson. I'll keep on fighting, but I feel like lying down in a bed and dying. I'm so full of things that I've had to suffer, so many sorrows. Marcos's case has been reported in ten different papers here and two in São Paulo. *Última Hora* reported that Marcos "had suffered an attack of motor paralysis after being 'interrogated.'" *A Tribuna* also said the same thing.

Letter from me to Marcos:

November 2, 1970

Finally I can give you some good news. My papers will be ready by the 16th. I will do everything possible to leave soon after. Now we just have to count the days, hours, and minutes. The news I've heard about you seems good, except regarding visits. I hope that we overcome this barrier soon. Hang on! I have worked a lot, and suffered a lot, and now I want to rest near you and do everything, EVERYTHING, to make things right. Have courage and faith!

Letter from my mother to me:

November 11, 1970

Marcos is doing well, but the neurological problems haven't disappeared. He's still fixated on that same idea; he's afraid of being returned to São Paulo or of being interrogated again, despite being told that it's not going to happen. Luciano, my brother-in-law who is a doctor, said that subconsciously this alone could keep him from improving.

Marcos later told me that the nurse assigned to his ward would come in every day and tell him: "Just wait. You'll see. Any day now you'll be sent back to São Paulo. Just wait." This terrorized him and made his situation worse. Because of these constant threats, he initiated a plan to appear even sicker than he was, so that he wouldn't be transferred back to São Paulo. After each meal he would stick his finger in his mouth to induce vomiting. So, in addition to all of the psychological and physical problems he was suffering, this left him even thinner and more fragile.

A letter from my mother added:

Mildo [Marcos's father—LPS] and I are going on Friday to meet with Brigadier Faria Lima, who is very interested in the case because of another young man who was also imprisoned and became friends with Marcos. This young man, who had worked with the Brigadier for five years, sought him out immediately after he was released. The Brigadier became concerned and even asked for a copy of Marcos's file from São Paulo. He said that the only thing that they have against Marcos is the accusations of the girl who was imprisoned the same day.

After my return to Washington in August, I immediately sought out a good friend who worked for the International Association of Machinists and Aerospace Workers. Jack Otero had been expelled from Brazil by the dictatorship as a persona non grata because, while in Brazil, he had protested against government repression of the labor movement. I told him what had happened to my son, and he wrote me a letter in response, saying that he had found influential friends in Washington who could help make the public in general more aware of Marcos's case. He also included an article by the journalist Jack Anderson that referred to the activities of one of the senators from Idaho regarding Brazil.*

When we met, Jack Otero counseled me on what I should do. He told me I should immediately begin the paperwork to become a naturalized citizen of the United States so that I could be protected. He also recommended that I write letters to Amnesty International in London, to the International Commission of Jurists in Switzerland, to the United Nations, and to the Organization of American States (OAS).

I immediately began my attack. On October 26, I wrote to Congressman Joel T. Broyhill of Virginia, indicating that I wanted to become a naturalized American citizen, and that I was under pressure because my twenty-nine-year-old son was suffering from motor paralysis and was begging for my presence. Because I had a green card, I was not allowed to spend very much time out of the country. Since I was already in the process of becoming a

---

* *Editor's note.* Jack Anderson was an investigative journalist who wrote the syndicated column "The Washington Merry-Go-Round" that published material about human rights violations in Latin America, among other issues. "One of the senators from Idaho" was the Democrat Frank Church, who was preparing hearings about U.S. government aid to Brazil.

naturalized citizen, I was only asking for him to help expedite my paperwork. Though he was a Republican and I was a Democrat, I had to go to him
because he was the U.S. Representative from the district of Virginia where
I was residing with my daughter Cristiana. He was wonderful, though, and
did everything he could for me.

I passed the language test and the test on general knowledge regarding
the United States, and I chose as a sponsor Tom Doherty, a marvelous and
faithful friend of our family. I was also asked to provide three letters of recommendation from people who knew me well. Thank God, I passed everything well. I had lived in the United States for more than five years, but the
naturalization process seemed to drag on because it was an election year.
Finally, I received a letter from the congressman's secretary informing me of
the naturalization meeting in Richmond, Virginia. On the appointed day,
I was very nervous as I made the long trip to Richmond. There were a lot
of other people from England, Latin America, Greece, and several other
countries that I can't remember. The room was overflowing. Each person
was asked to name the country they had come from. Afterward, with our
hands over our hearts, we all pledged allegiance to the American flag and
promised not to commit any crime against the government. The tears ran
down my face. Although I love the United States, I had never had the intention of giving up my ancestors' nationality. (My dear grandfather had always
been so proud of his country! Oh, what we won't do for a child!) Following
this, there was a reception with many hugs and congratulations. I received a
nice certificate, and it was official. Now I just had to receive a passport, and
I could go to Brazil!

Ron Smith, an American who had accompanied one of the Brazilian
groups that we translated for, told me that Marcos's case was under review
at a very high level within the American government, but he couldn't reveal
how he knew.

On October 15, Amnesty International responded to me by letter from
Philadelphia. "How wonderful," I thought, "to feel their support. Surely
things are going to improve." The members of this group are angels. I hope
they know how much they did for my son.

For those who don't know, throughout the world Amnesty International
organizes small groups of volunteers interested in helping political prisoners

who have been tortured and unjustly imprisoned. They publish reports on the situation of each country and pressure governments and other international groups on behalf of individual and social human rights.

"Our" group was from Philadelphia. Amnesty International assigned them to our case. The group was made up of fourteen people who performed an important role in helping Marcos. Each member of the group wrote letters to the Brazilian president, ministers, officials of the Supreme Military Court, the vice-president, etc. In short, they bombarded the government with letters asking: "Where is Marcos Arruda? Why has he disappeared? What did he do to deserve this? Why has he been hospitalized if he was always in good health? Why has he been imprisoned without being charged in any court of law? Etc., etc."

A general responded to these letters, claiming that Marcos was subversive and saying where he was being detained. This was sufficient for Técio to begin legal action! The general's response was the proof we needed, for before this point there had been no legal or official record that Marcos was even imprisoned. The general's letter helped us immensely. He even sent one of his assistants to inquire about whether Técio was familiar with Amnesty International and if they should be given a formal response. This was the icing on the cake. Técio immediately replied that it was a very important organization, one to which the government ought to respond in order to avoid a scandal. We were all thrilled with Técio!

Soon after this, I read in the *Washington Post* that a priest named Louis Michael Colonnese was horrified by the news of the terrible acts being committed in the torture chambers of Latin America and that he was going to ask for the Pope's intervention against this flagrant disregard for the law. On October 28, I sent him a letter recounting our situation and I included a copy of the letter I had sent to Minister Buzaid. I soon received a reply, and I sent him another letter, dated November 6, in which I informed him that my mother had been able to see Marcos for one hour. I also advised him that I was leaving for Rio on November 18 and that, as a naturalized American citizen, I was going to see if I could force the American consul to visit Marcos.

So with all the courage I could muster, I made my way back to Brazil. I left a statement in the United States, however, in case I was detained by the police in Brazil. All of the "dangerous" correspondence I had carried on, such as letters to international organizations and to Father Colonnese, I had placed between two pages of a Vogue magazine which I had glued shut to hide while I went through Brazilian customs. I wanted to appear "clean" to the authorities. My fear was that they would seize everything, but I entered with my new passport without any problems.

On November 20, the day I arrived in Brazil, I went running to see Marcos. I was trembling with emotion. This is what I wrote in a letter to Father Colonnese the next day:

Letter from me to Father Colonnese:

Rio, November 21, 1970

He was alone in an enormous infirmary, which was completely tiled and cold. I had the same nauseating feeling as before. I went from the Security Office to meet with the Captain, then on to meet the General, after which I met the Doctor and finally, Marcos. The Captain is a tall and ugly man with the face of a hippopotamus. He treated me as if I didn't exist.

When we entered, Marcos was alone and experiencing full convulsions! The guard yelled, "Wait!" But I responded by pushing through the door and yelling, "I'm not waiting for anything!" and I ran to Marcos's side. Mônica, who had come with me, called to the Captain, "Please, please, he's having an attack!" The Captain shrugged, turned, and left.

I held Marcos in my arms, crying and calling to him, "Marcos, my son, my dear Marcos, my son, it's me, your mother! Come back, my son, come back to me!" It was horrible. His body twisted in strong and uncontrollable convulsions, and his teeth clamped shut. He was trembling all over. I held him tightly and said, "Please, my son, my dear son." Mônica was crying. The security guard was crying too. Slowly, Marcos wrapped his arms around my neck as the convulsions began to diminish. Then he too began crying, "Oh, it's so wonderful to have you back. I'm so glad you've come."

When after some time he finally calmed down and we were all able to stop crying, he complained of a severe headache.

The Captain had only given us an hour. The doctor, Dr. Boia, another SOB, reduced our time to twenty minutes. They said Marcos wasn't feeling well, that some of the food he had received from his grandmother had made him sick. He threw up everything he tried to eat.

With only a few minutes to talk alone, we used a trick we had thought of earlier. Mônica began speaking in a very loud voice, telling him all about the party they had had when I had left Washington. At the same time, I softly spoke with him about more serious matters concerning what we were doing to get him released. He motioned to me by putting his finger in his mouth that he did not want to return to São Paulo. He was terrified of being returned and was forcing himself to throw up to prevent them from sending him back. He held me tightly, saying, "Please don't let them take me back!"

I promised to take every step possible. The hospital had asked us to bring him some crutches so that he could begin to walk. We thought it was so that they could hasten his return to São Paulo, so we didn't bring them. They also told us that his health wasn't so bad and that he could walk with crutches or some other support. They said his leg was improving but that his eye was still closed. We had brought him a beautiful poster and a robe, but we were not allowed to give them to him. He was dirty, unshaven, very pale, and weak.

I told him about you, Mike, and we showed him the medal from the Pope. He was very surprised and grateful.

He still has about five convulsions a day. He told us that he fell from his bed during two of them, had come to on the ground, and had hit his head hard. He had been improving with some of the epilepsy medicine, but he said that after the diagnosis came in that he wasn't epileptic, those idiots at the hospital took him off the medicine, saying that in the opinion of the hospital it was too dangerous. He is very depressed and afraid.

After an agonizing twenty minutes, two soldiers, a captain, and a security guard escorted us out of the hospital. I guess we are obviously very dangerous.

Inside I was totally depressed and in a panic. The infirmary is large, with around twenty beds. It's very cold, and he is there by himself in a bed in the middle of the room. This alone makes me sick.

I immediately went to the American Embassy and spoke with the Consul General. I gave him my report and emphasized the importance of taking some action before Monday, the date that he thought he might be transferred. The Consul General is a very reserved man. He hardly said anything. He had to leave to attend a political meeting, but it wasn't long before he returned. He gave me some advice, and then said he would phone me later. We still haven't heard anything from him!

I also spoke to the Labor Attaché, who promised that he would meet with the consul to work on our case. Técio said that it would be really good if we could demonstrate that the United States government was interested.

I then went to see Dom Aloísio Lorscheider, the Archbishop of Rio de Janeiro. He was wonderful and compassionate and seemed to be very interested. He said that he wouldn't be able to see Marcos in person because he would lose his connections with the government, as well as the trust that he had gained that allowed him to help many other people like us. He then pounded his fist on the table and said, "They have feet of clay. Their time will come."

On Sunday, Dom Lorscheider phoned me and said that Dom Alberto Trevisan, the Auxiliary Bishop of Rio, had gone to visit Marcos on Saturday morning on behalf of the Archbishop, but they would not allow him to enter!

At least it was a step forward!

Dom Lorscheider also said, "They are all beasts. The President really wants more moderate policies; and, if they could get rid of Canavarro, Rademaker and Sarmento,* we would all be saved. The rumor is, though, that he already asked Canavarro to resign, but he refused to do so, so don't be surprised if one of these days you wake up and the streets are filled with tanks and the government is in the hands of someone as bad as Hitler." This only confirmed my suspicions that it's not the President who's giving the orders.

I went to the home of my sister and called Malcolm Hallam. He was the American Consul in São Paulo at the time, but he had been my supervisor when I worked at the American Consulate in Rio from 1957 to 1958. He was shocked by my description of what I had seen, and he offered to speak with the Consul in Rio immediately.

These were all good leads for getting Marcos out, I thought.

Elza and I then went to the Ministry of War to see a certain captain. He wasn't in, but we spoke with a public relations officer. He sat by my side and took notes on everything we said. He told us that he had heard people talking about Marcos's case. Look at the lack of communication among them, and how they do everything in secret! I watched him write:

1. Doesn't want to return to São Paulo. [Underlined by LPS.]

2. Under contract with the State Department.

He wrote this as I was saying to him, "I was so shocked after spending so many years in the United States to return and find Brazil in this state: the lack of freedom, no habeas corpus, torture, and not even a private doctor or my own lawyer has been allowed to see him."

He wrote and wrote.

We returned to my sister's home where we learned that my brother-in-law, Luciano de Britto Pereira, who is a doctor and had been a colleague of the hospital director where Marcos was staying, had gone to see Marcos. He too was not allowed to enter; he was only permitted to look from the door (some consolation!), despite being very well re-

---

* *Editor's note.* In 1969, General José Canavarro Pereira was in charge of Operation OBAN in São Paulo. That same year in September, Admiral Augusto Rademaker assumed a caretaker presidency with two other members of the armed forces when President Costa e Silva suffered a stroke. At the time General Siseno Sarmento headed the First Army in Rio de Janeiro. All three represented the hard-line rightwing of the military regime.

ceived by General Galleno. He was allowed to see Marcos's file, which at least said, "psychological disturbances from fear of being tortured."

The next day I went to speak, for the first time, with Colonel Octávio Medeiros, Luciano's brother-in-law, at the Laranjeiras Palace.* I was so exhausted that I didn't know whether I should thank him for what he had already done or pretend that I didn't know anything.

He was gracious and asked me to give him a complete report of everything I knew about the case, along with my honest opinion. I wrote a report, and I offered to write and sign another statement saying that I would be responsible for Marcos. If they would permit him to return home to be treated by our own doctors, I would make sure that he obeyed all orders until his case had been heard in the courts. I also declared that we were anxious to return to the United States where I worked in order to resolve our financial problems and also to take care of his health. All of this was according to Técio's advice.

The Colonel finally excused himself, saying, "I will do everything I can to free your son."

We later learned that Marcos was never seen by any specialists and that the hospital had lied to us. The beast of a doctor there is not even qualified to care for him—he's a dermatologist.

Marcos has a strong spirit, but the horrors continue.

A good friend of his was in Montevideo and saw Marcos's name on the first page of one of the newspapers there, along with his entire story. No one knows who gave them the story—could it have been Amnesty International?

We have also been able to obtain the names of the leaders of the torture teams: Captains Dauro Cirillo, Faria, Maurício Lopes Lima, Homero Cesar Machado, Benoni de Arruda Albernaz, and Lt. Col. Waldir Coelho, who was the head of OBAN at the time. They are all very well known, and they are the ones who gave Marcos his "treatment," as they call it.

Mônica saw one of them, at the hospital in São Paulo, leaving Marcos's cell. She went in after they left and found Marcos with a red and swollen face.

* *Editor's note.* The Laranjeiras Palace was a former presidential residency in Rio de Janeiro that was used for official federal government activities during the military regime.

It is possible that they had beaten him. Thank God that Marcos can't even remember that this happened. He also doesn't recall many other abuses he suffered that other prisoners claimed to have witnessed.

The letter to Father Colonnese continues:

I have few hopes, for our lawyer has warned me that they can do whatever they want with him. The same way that they nearly killed him, they can keep him in custody without a trial or demand that he be permanently detained. They are the law!

Well, my good dear friend, I'll stop here. As soon as I have more news, I'll write again.

Please, keep praying for my son.

The Tribulations of Other Prisoners

The days passed by without any news except what we were hearing about other prisoners. Meanwhile, I kept writing letters to the United States. Técio told us that the lawyer Augusto Sussekind de Moraes Rego had been imprisoned along with two other important people. They were thrown in jail, their heads covered with hoods, and they were given food mixed with manure. At the time Sussekind de Moraes Rego was seventy years old and was a member of the Federal Council of the Brazilian Bar Association. After three days and a big uproar, they were finally released.

We also heard a story that General Lott, who was once a presidential candidate, had a grandson in the same situation as Marcos's. The general dressed in his formal uniform and went to see his grandson. When he arrived, the major on duty said that he couldn't see him. The general pulled out his revolver and shot the officer five times! I don't know if this was true, but these are the stories we heard in Brazil at the time. I was so jealous of the general in that moment! But I knew that I would be more useful working "on the outside." To this end, I continued feeding the Philadelphia Amnesty International group with such stories. They continued to barrage the military leaders with letters asking for information on Marcos. The military must have been surprised that these Americans knew so many details of what was going on in Brazil . . . until one day, when this backfired on us, as will be seen.

At the time, though, we heard about case after case of others who had been imprisoned and tortured.

Hugo Moreno was an Argentine who was in the same cell as Marcos while he was in the Second Army Hospital in São Paulo. When I visited Marcos during my first trip back to Brazil, Hugo slipped me two small notes, written on toilet paper, asking for help. He said that no one in the world knew he was there, that his legs were paralyzed, and that he was suffering from internal bleeding from being brutally tortured.

As soon as I returned to Rio, I wrote a letter to the Argentine Consulate in which I included the two notes and explained how I had received them. I took them to the embassy in person, but it was an Argentine holiday and the building was locked. So, I left them under the door, and, thank God, everything turned out well. One day much later, through a coincidence, Marcos and I were in Lisbon at the same time. Marcos said that he was going to give me a surprise, and he took me to a street corner. I looked up and a young man was running toward us. He took me in his arms and exclaimed, "You saved my life. You were the one!" It was Hugo. He had been freed by the Argentine Consulate and had subsequently moved to Paris.

Another terrible story that I was told from official sources is about three young women. We knew one of them, Márcia Savagé. She was a friend of my daughters' and used to come by our house. She and the other two young women were imprisoned somewhere just outside of Rio. The Supreme Court granted them their freedom. Their mothers, along with their lawyer, went to a meeting place to pick them up around six o'clock in the evening, but they didn't appear until early in the morning. Just as they arrived, three cars drove up, and nine men jumped out. They grabbed the lawyer and threw him to the ground. Then they seized the young women and sped off again! This was the "hard line" military in action. Their case returned to the courts. Finally, they were found in the prisons again and were forced to repeat the entire process. In November 1970, they were granted asylum by the Chilean Embassy, and they made their way to Chile.

Letter from me to Father Colonnese:

Rio, December 28, 1970

When your letter arrived, I was at the point of desperation. It was truly a balm, bringing hope and support, for I was beginning to feel abandoned in my fight.

After I wrote you the first letter, we received permission to see Marcos Tuesday mornings from 9:30 to 10:30 for three weeks. I said to him, "As soon as you're better, we'll get you out of here." He improved so fast that it was astonishing. His eye stayed closed, but the last time I saw him, he was walking without crutches, though his leg was very swollen from so much exercise. His spirits were high.

He gave me several notes saying that he was very worried about a young woman across the corridor from his cell. (Marcos is always thinking of others.) She had been taken to the hospital because of severe hemorrhaging, the result of a miscarriage she suffered after having been badly tortured and beaten. She was only twenty-one years old. They knew she was pregnant, but they were looking for her husband and had brought her in to try to force her to say where he was hiding. I have written a letter to her family and am doing everything I can to help her get out as well.

In the letter I was referring to Estrella Bohadana, a young woman who worked with one of the labor unions in Volta Redonda. Her story is related in the letter Marcos wrote to the Pope, dated February 4, 1971.

The Big Visit

Continuing my letter to Father Colonnese

Marcos keeps asking to see the lawyer, so I asked him to come. We came in a group: Técio Lins e Silva, the American Consul, my other son Miguel Arruda, my ex-husband and me. We arrived at the hospital unannounced. The hospital director, General Galleno, froze when he saw us! I clearly read in his expression and the lines of his face that he had been cornered. He greeted us politely explaining that it wasn't his decision whether or not we could see Marcos, but rather that it was a question of security. He then excused himself to make a telephone call.

Shortly thereafter a security officer from the army police arrived. He was in dress uniform and nervously tapped his baton against his leg as he told us that he could not permit us to visit Marcos. He sent us instead to the police headquarters at the Ministry of War. We left downtrodden, but since it was nearby and we were all together, I asked if we could all go. They agreed, and so we made our way there.

Upon entering we were met at the door by Colonel Mello, who was extremely ill mannered. He was a small man, dressed in a cavalry uniform, and he had a diagonal scar on his face. Técio explained why we were there, and the colonel tersely replied, "Surely you must know that to receive this kind of permission you have to speak with the court authorities." Técio responded, "There is no record of where Marcos is imprisoned in any court in the country." The colonel's response, "That's not my problem."

We introduced the American Consul and the others, explaining that I was an American and was worried about the well-being of my son. The Colonel said, "The rights of Americans end where the rights of Brazilians begin." Hearing this, the Consul became red in the face—he had just come from Portugal and understood Portuguese very well.

We again left disheartened, but despite our failure, I was comforted to believe that at least the presence of the Consul and Técio would give them reason enough not to harm my son any further.

I wrote the statement taking responsibility that I had promised to Colonel Medeiros and sent it to him. Soon after, we received wonderful news. He had asked his own mother to telephone my mother, saying that Marcos would be home by Christmas. This news made us so happy and hopeful!

Our constant visits to the hospital, along with the interest of our friends and relatives, finally resulted in Marcos being treated like a human being. Marcos had also made friends among the attendants and employees of the hospital.

On November 8, we went back to the hospital and, to the last man—from the general director of the hospital, to Captain Morais, to the Security officers, and even the sergeant—everyone told us that Marcos was going to be released to go home. They said that two police officers from São Paulo had come to see him, and he had given them a long statement, "which pleased them." The chief of police, that Mello fellow, had said to him in person, "As soon as you walk, you're going home."

Our hopes were lifted. We began planning for our Christmas Eve dinner. I got his room ready and put the beautiful medal [from the Pope] you sent Marcos on his pillow. The air was filled with euphoria as we began decorating the house for Christmas in preparation for Marcos's return.

Chapter Eleven

I also tried telepathy. "Dear Pope, pay heed, you have to bring my son home, TODAY."

For five days in a row, Miguel and I parked and waited in front of the hospital because we were afraid that Marcos might be released and then immediately kidnapped again by the "hard liners," just as Márcia Savagé had been. We spent hours and hours waiting, listening to the radio, talking and sleeping in the car. Finally, Miguel said, "Mom, I'm sorry, but I have to work." So we stopped going to wait for him outside the hospital.

At the bottom of my heart, I knew that it didn't matter anyway because a police vehicle could drive into the hospital, pick him up, and leave without our seeing anything.

And that is what happened . . .

On December 22, Marcos was taken far from the hospital to the DOI-CODI, the headquarters of the military police. We only learned of his transfer because of the goodness of the hospital director, General Galleno.

We went there immediately, Miguel, his father, Mônica, and I. We were met at the door, just as at the General Headquarters, by a young soldier who said, "We cannot tell you anything. You must go to the General Headquarters or to the Ministry of War." We insisted, and he made a phone call. We were soon met by a man wearing a shirt on which his nametag was covered with tape, a common practice among the torturers so that they're not identified. He asked my ex-husband to write what he wanted on a piece of paper. He then left, and we waited for what felt like an eternity, until another soldier returned to us with the same piece of paper. On the back was written: "Go to the Ministry of War, room—." We telephoned the ministry to see if we would be received, but we were given no response other than to wait. We then returned home very depressed.

This was perhaps the most difficult moment of our ordeal. The 23rd of December came, and then the 24th. While our turkey roasted in the oven, all we could do was sit and cry. Then, out of the blue on Christmas Eve, my mother called, "A sergeant just called and told me that Marcos has returned to the hospital!" My heart sank, "Oh my God! They've tortured him again!"

The Saga Continues

A moment later, we were called by the same sergeant. I cried into the phone: "What happened? What happened? Was he tortured again? Please tell me!" The man calmly responded, "No, ma'am, he was having convulsions and was sent to the hospital because of this. He asked me to call and wish you a Merry Christmas."

We later learned from Marcos that, after being there for three days and hearing the cries of those being tortured at night, and without his medication, he began having convulsions.

Continuing my letter to Father Colonnese:

The next day, I returned to the hospital to deliver more of Marcos's convulsion medication. I was met by a young man who claimed to be a doctor, but whose name tag was also covered with tape. I told him that if Marcos did not receive this medication, his condition would worsen.

He responded rudely, asking, "Who told you that he is here? You are not supposed to know that."

"It was the hospital director who telephoned me," I said.

"That's absurd," he yelled and then stormed off.

I cried inside, "Oh, my dear Brazil, what have they done to you? Who are these monsters, and where have they come from? Do they have mothers?" As the uniformed soldiers at the hospital entrance clicked their heels to salute higher-ranking officers, I could only think of the Gestapo.

On Christmas day, I telephoned Colonel Medeiros in Brasília. He was shocked to learn that Marcos hadn't been released. He said that he had spoken with his cousin, Colonel Paiva, and entrusted him with Marcos's case here in Rio. I telephoned Colonel Paiva, but he was gone for the weekend. I telephoned again on Monday, but he didn't know what was going on and had thought that Marcos had spent Christmas at home with us. He asked us to call back around five o'clock, and that in the meantime he would take care of things. We did as he said and called back at five. His secretary gave us the following answer: "Colonel Paiva left on a trip and will only return next week . . ."

Once again, my suspicion was confirmed that the president of the republic held no power over anyone in the military. General Sarmento and his gang would not respect the direct orders of the Office of the President to release Marcos before Christmas. Our holiday was one of tears and sadness.

On Tuesday, we went to the hospital again. It had been three weeks since we had last seen Marcos. Captain Morais informed us that all visits were cancelled due to the kidnapping of the German Ambassador. He said that Marcos was fine, and that he had been surprised to see him back. He had been gone for Christmas and had thought that Marcos was being released. He also said, laughing ironically, that if the problem with the kidnapping lasted for ten years, then we wouldn't see Marcos for ten years, as if this were the funniest thing in the world. He sent us again to see the infamous Colonel Mello.

This time, the colonel asked us to sit. He said that Marcos would have gone home on the 22nd, but they received a call from São Paulo ordering them to stop everything. That's why he was still there.

"But he is quite well," he said.

"No, he's not," I responded. "He's already begun having convulsions again in the hospital."

The colonel nearly fell out of his chair!

"He's in the hospital? But, I was not informed of this?!"

He was so surprised that he could hardly control his response. In short, everything is a mess and completely disorganized!

Colonel Mello has no idea who Colonel Medeiros is, and, for his part, Colonel Medeiros has no idea who is disobeying his orders, as he added indignantly, "But it was a direct order from the president!"

If it's true that someone from São Paulo made the telephone call, then someone there is doing whatever he wants to, without asking anyone. The military police were not communicating with Colonel Mello, their commander within the Ministry of War. It's sickening, irritating, and frustrating. You can be sure, Mike, that I have always been a pacifist, but this has given me the urge to grab a revolver and begin shooting at anything moving in a green uniform! This is what they are doing to every family that is suffering similar injustices and humiliations. Violence creates violence.

Today I spent the entire day trying to call São Paulo to speak with

Colonel Albuquerque, who helped me so much there. I also tried to reach Colonel Medeiros in Brasília but was unsuccessful. And here in Rio, I tried contacting General Siseno Sarmento, who is known to be the overlord of cruelty and coercion within the military and who is said to be untouchable.

If we are unsuccessful this time, it will be the last . . .

One of the conditions of Marcos's release is that he will have to stay in Rio for a long period of time. Thus, our plan of leaving soon after for the United States has been sunk. Even so, I am going to stay in contact with the Consul, in case there is a change in government, in order to request political asylum. The rumors continue to circulate that the hard liners are going to openly seize control of the country.

I hope I haven't been too confusing by giving you so much detail. All of this is flying around my mind, together with faces and feelings of revulsion, and nights of insomnia.

The problem is that right now within the military and the government there is a game of push and pull as they vie among themselves for trust, loyalty, power, and control. And, along with this, there is the fear of offending whoever will rise to power tomorrow.

Thank you so much for your help and affectionate interest.

. . .

P.S. The family thinks that my letter should not be published in any newspapers because it might end up hurting Marcos's chances of being released.

Time went on, and they continued to prohibit our visits. Marcos remained in custody, and all our efforts to see him were in vain. We tried to keep up his spirits by sending in small notes of comfort:

From me:

Dear Son:

Our fight goes on as always. There is no end to the love we feel for you, and we anxiously await your release. May God grant that it is not far off.

All of my love, Mom.

From Miguel and Lúcia:

Getting you out has been so hard and sad. I am certain that '71 will bring you to us again. Everything is ready for you. We love you so much, and we're dying to see you. We are with you always, from the bottom of our hearts. We love you.

From my mother:

Because of the uncertainty of being able to see you, I didn't go this time. But, I'm going to go out today to fight for your release. I pray always, always for you.

Here is a copy of my letter to the coordinator of Amnesty International in Philadelphia, dated January 2, 1971:

Dear Mr. Baurys,

Please see the enclosed copy of a letter I was obliged to write in order to save the life of my son Marcos. Please keep it close at hand in case a Brazilian authority contacts you by phone or by letter. If they ask, tell them that, at my request, you have already destroyed your files on Marcos.

Unfortunately, your last letter to them caused more harm than good. Please understand that I am not writing to criticize. We had to try every means of defense.

Marcos was to have been freed on December 22. On that day, he was taken to the headquarters of the military police and asked to sign a statement releasing the government of all responsibility before he was allowed to return home. We waited and waited. He never came! After fighting, praying, and running from one place to the other, from colonel to colonel, we discovered that he had been sent back to the Army Hospital on Christmas Eve, suffering convulsions.

(In reality, he had returned to the hospital only on Christmas day. At that time, we didn't know anything regarding the "treatment" he had received by the military police, and we only learned of what happened from Marcos himself after he was released.)

Since the kidnapping of the German Ambassador, we haven't seen him. We are told that he is well and that he is walking. We have learned from relatives close to General Siseno Sarmento, the commander of the First Army in Rio, that Marcos is not being allowed to go home because they have learned that he has been sending information to Philadelphia. I understood immediately. So I wrote the enclosed letter, translated into Portuguese, together with the letter to the General, explaining that I was the "guilty" person who, out of desperation, had contacted Amnesty International when I was alone in the United States and that, after speaking with a lawyer, I was advised to write to you as I have done.

I say in my letter that I am unaware of the content of any of the letters you have written to them. I only know that you have written letters asking for Marcos's freedom. They are upset because you accuse the Brazilian government in your letter.

As soon as I am able to arrange a meeting with the General, which I am trying to achieve through three different people, I will telegraph you the following: "Everything is cool. Please, write." Which will mean: "Marcos is free!"

Chapter Twelve

At that point, write them a polite letter, thanking them for their quick action and for recognizing that it was just [on their part to release him—ed.]. Praise them a little so that they will leave us in peace.

If I am successful, then we will begin the second phase of our plan: to convince them to allow me to bring Marcos to the United States. Please forgive my poor typing. I've been "out of it" today.

While this was going on, I sought out a woman, the owner of a boutique in town, whose daughter was married to one of General Sarmento's sons. She promised to talk to her daughter so that she could speak to the General on our behalf. I had been recommended to her by a relative of my daughter-in-law, through a friend of a comedian who is a good friend of the General.

On January 7, 1971, we received the following letter:

Dear Mrs. Sattamini,

I am directed to acknowledge the letter which you recently addressed to the Holy Father.

I am glad to inform you that your petition has been duly transmitted to the Apostolic Nuncio in Rio de Janeiro, with a request that the matter be given every possible attention.

His Holiness gives assurance of his prayers for you and your son in this difficult moment.

With my prayerful good wishes, I remain

Sincerely yours in Christ,

J. Benelli

Secretary to the Vatican State

On that same day we received news from our friends in Philadelphia:

Dear Mrs. Sattamini:

I received a telephone call from Cristiana Arruda on Monday, January 4. She passed on your instructions to stop writing letters and to avoid publicity. We will follow your instructions. I also wrote to Amnesty International in London and suggested that they heed your new instructions.

I understand from Miss Arruda that Marcos was to be released at

Christmas but was not because the authorities used the excuse that there was too much publicity in this case. I know that must have been a terribly frustrating blow to you and Marcos. That is an inexcusably cruel act to add to their already long list. Of course, it goes without saying that we wish for success in your continuing efforts to gain Marcos's release.

For the record, Amnesty International has officially "adopted" Marcos as a "prisoner of conscience."

Did you receive my letter with enclosure dated December 4, 1970?

Please keep in touch and excuse the brevity of this note.

Take care and good luck.

Very truly, yours,

Stanley D. Baurys

On January 12, 1971, we received another letter from the Philadelphia Amnesty International group:

I received your letter dated January 2, 1971, with enclosure on January 11, 1971. I understand your instructions perfectly, and I will follow them to the letter.

I appreciate your thanks for our "interest," but I'm afraid that after my last letter to Gen. Braga, we've been more of a hindrance than a "help." I am terribly, terribly sorry that they are still keeping Marcos; apparently because of that letter. I really feel very badly about it. As you know, the letter was written on December 2. They must have told you that they would release Marcos by Christmas, sometime in early or mid-December. I wonder if they changed their mind sometime between December 5 and Christmas and did not tell you simply to harass you. Perhaps they really did not intend to release him at that particular time. Maybe they feel that if they frustrate you enough, that even you might give up trying—if only temporarily. Of course, I know that that would never happen, but maybe they think it will. Then again, perhaps they really are afraid of public opinion in this particular case. You would know all of this better than I. Also, perhaps the "kidnapping" of the Swiss diplomat influenced their decision. Perhaps they feel that they should not release any prisoners at all during this sensitive period. I really was angered and frustrated by the news conveyed in your last letter. I wish that I could do something more tangible.

I believe that I've already told you that I have notified Amnesty International in London telling them to refrain from publicizing the case.

I have enclosed copies of the other letters that I have sent to various officials. The one that I marked "Form Letter" was sent to the President of Brazil and the Ministers of Justice, Interior, Foreign, Finance, and Education. It was also sent to the State Governors of Guanabara and São Paulo. Each one received the letter on three different occasions; late October, late November; and late December (I did not receive the phone call until January 4). It was sent to General Braga on only one occasion in early November. [. . .—LPS]

If you want me to get in touch with someone in the USA, please let me know.

I eagerly await your next communication.

Again—I'm sorry for what happened.

Yours affectionately,

Stan Baurys

P.S. I also sent a letter to the Brazilian Embassy in Washington, D.C. Of course, other members of our group have sent letters similar to those enclosed.

Letter from my mother to Marcos:

Rio, January 22, 1971

It has been crazy and difficult to get through the last few days. We live in the hope that you will be released soon, but the days pass by and nothing happens. Many times God tries our faith and our trust in Him in these things. We shouldn't become discouraged but trust in His goodness and hope.

You were not allowed to leave only because of your state of health when you had a relapse at the military police prison. [My mother was not aware of the other information we had received.—LPS] Colonel Mello, the chief of the military police, told me that they are waiting for you to get better. At the hospital they've told us that you are much better, that you're walking, and they are only waiting for your vision to improve. [More lies they fed my mother.—LPS]

I haven't rested a single day during my fight for you, and we hope that you will soon be freed . . .

Letters from Marcos's father to Marcos:

January 15, 1971

I came to see you today (Friday) to bring you some food and find out what's going on. We have been told that you are getting better each day! May God protect you! We just have to hold on for a little longer till we are together again!

January 19, 1971

May God bless you. We came to visit you today to bring you our love and concern. Many prayers have been offered for your freedom, which we feel is very close . . .

January 23, 1971

Today, Saturday afternoon, I came again to give you my support and the love of a father who misses you, who is waiting anxiously but patiently for your release. The more we suffer today, the greater our joy will be tomorrow. May God bless you through your father . . .

At the same time, we received tidbits of information from the hospital that turned out to be lies. Our dashed hopes that he would be leaving soon left our family despondent.

Letter from me to Stanley Baurys:

Rio, January 22, 1971
Dear Mr. Baurys,

Please don't feel badly about what has happened. You are doing what is right, and so am I. I am also sure that Marcos would be the first one to approve of it and would be willing to face one more month there, if it could help other people, as well, in the long run.

As I wrote you before and my daughter Cristiana today, telling her to call you about many details. These are excuses that they are giving. Each day there is a new one. The last one is: "My boss decided that he is not well yet and must remain in the hospital for further treatment." That's what Colonel Mello, Chief of Police of the First Army said. He also told my mother that he did not like me, because I made threats to take this case to the OAS.

This only shows you how badly informed he is. I not only made threats; I sent letters to every single organization that I thought would help.

I think that your form letters to all those authorities are excellent. One thing is for certain now: they won't touch him again, not after this publicity.

Is it true that in one of the letters you wrote to some authority about Marcos you included another one, in the same envelope, about somebody else? This is another excuse for delaying the case: the dossiers were mixed up. The other person, according to them, is a bank robber and terrorist . . . (so was Marcos to them, until they found out otherwise, but it was too late).

They changed their minds about releasing Marcos on December 22, when he started having convulsions again. (Before that they said there was a "problem" in São Paulo, which wasn't true at all.)

General Galleno has shown interest in letting us see Marcos, and he told me that if it were up to him, he would be home by now. He never mentioned your letter, but I am sure it helped. He is extremely polite to us.

However, no visits are allowed yet, although Colonel Mello insists that permission was given on Tuesday, January 19. They say it is the red tape that delays moving papers from one office to the other.

Please get in touch with Cristiana, she has all the last details.

Well my friend, I'm not discouraged, because I have a plan for future action. Therefore, keep your spirit high and keep up with the good work. Just wait for my telegram. It might come earlier than we think, right? It is gratifying to know that you all care. Thank you again.

Yours fondly.

When I left Washington, D.C., on November 19, 1970, I gave my daughter Cristiana instructions that if I should disappear or be imprisoned in Brazil, she should send a statement that I had prepared to the *Washington Post*, the State Department, the UN, the OAS, the White House, Amnesty International, and the International Commission of Jurists in Geneva.

Inspired by James Bond films, my overactive imagination created scenes in which I would climb to the top of a building and threaten to jump unless my son were released. Or, I would imagine the Marines arriving in a helicopter at night and breaking into the hospital prison to rescue my son. Our situation in Rio, however, eventually reached the point at which these "flights of imagination," as I called them, were much closer to reality than not.

I wrote a letter on January 28, 1971, with the intention of sending it to every authority I could think of, every international organization related to human rights, and to every religious institution, if Marcos weren't released within the next five days:

> My name is Lina Penna Sattamini. I am a naturalized American.
>
> Today, I am beginning a hunger strike to save my son, Marcos Penna Sattamini de Arruda, who has been imprisoned and hospitalized since May 11, 1970, after having been brutally tortured by the military police in São Paulo at the headquarters for the Bandeirantes Operation.
>
> I have exhausted every "proper" and "prudent" channel available in Brazil today . . . (lawyers, letters, lobbyists, etc.).
>
> Since I arrived in Rio on November 19, 1970, I have only seen my son three times. We have not been allowed to see Marcos since the

kidnapping of the Swiss Ambassador on December 8, despite an order from the Supreme Military Court permitting visitors!

My family and I have spoken with high authorities close to the President of the Republic, within the Second Army in São Paulo, and in the First Army in Rio, asking and pleading for the liberation of my sick son, based on the fact that he is not guilty of what he has been accused of [terrorism — ed.], and because of the fact that he is very ill, suffering convulsions and psychological trauma. The very authorities of the military hospital in São Paulo and the military hospital in Rio, where he is now being held, have declared many times that as long as Marcos remains imprisoned away from the love, security, and care of his family, his condition will not improve.

We have learned through reliable official sources that Marcos was granted his freedom on December 2, 1970, by President Médici himself. These papers were signed again and reissued in Rio on January 8, 1971.

Yet Marcos remains imprisoned in the hospital, cut off from any outside contact and without any idea of when he will be allowed to leave. He should be a free citizen! He spent Christmas and New Years in prison, incommunicado, even though he was supposed to be freed!

I am tired of pleading!

I want to offer myself as a sacrifice in exchange for my son's freedom.

I want Marcos to be delivered to me at the American Embassy, with a passport and permission to leave Brazil.

I will take him to the United States, where he can recover in peace and return to being a useful and productive person who enjoys the simple right to exist.

A copy of this letter is in the hands of my daughter in Washington, D.C. If my demands are not met, she will send this letter to every American, European, and Latin American newspaper, as well as to the international organizations that are already aware of this case.

If you allow me to die, then I will be but one more victim of a country that tortures innocent people for political purposes. O Brazil, my dear Brazil, whom I love and whom I see suffering because of unscrupulous hands!

I think of all the parents who, like me, are suffering the anguish and horror of seeing their children crippled at the hands of these barbarous torturers, yet who remain silent in their humiliation, hoping that a "kangaroo court" will resolve their uncertain destiny. It's time to fight!

On February 1, 1971, three days after delivering my ultimatum, and just as I was departing by plane for work in Brasília as a translator at a meeting of the General Assembly of the OAS, Marcos was released in front of the Ministry of War. They left him on President Vargas Avenue without a dime. Moments before he was released, he had been allowed to call his grandmother to tell her that he was on his way to her home. He had a final interview with the fearsome Colonel Mello, who told him he knew he was an "irrecoverable subversive" and that, if he made a single misstep, he and his mother, who had created so many problems, would pay for it.

Marcos was afraid of being kidnapped again as he left, thus the telephone call to his grandmother was a small guarantee of safety. He took a taxi directly to her house on Voluntários da Patria Street in Botafogo. As he left the taxi, he noticed what seemed to be a police ambulance parked across the street that left only after Marcos had entered the house.

They called me that night with the news; and I nearly fainted with joy, yet I also felt frustrated and even punished by the conclusion of this entire odyssey I had been living. I was devastated that I had not been there the moment Marcos was released, to take my son in my arms now that he was finally free.

In Brasília, I was staying with an old friend from Washington, D.C., who was also participating in the OAS conference. I had an aunt living in Brasília, but I thought it would be more practical to stay with my friend, seeing as we could go to the conference together each day. As soon as we returned home after the first session of the conference, I received the phone call telling me of Marcos's release. I spoke with Marcos and felt exalted and filled with joy! Afterwards, my friend asked me, "So what exactly happened to Marcos?" I then told her everything in detail from the beginning. As soon as I finished she got up and ran to the bathroom and threw up. I felt so bad, believing that she was so sensitive that it was hard for her to hear the truth. She then excused herself and went to bed early.

The next day, she got up and left before I could see her. I had to make my way to the conference on my own. The same thing happened at the end of the day. She left before I could find her, and I had to find my own way back to her house. When I finally arrived, she was sitting waiting for me. I was startled by her serious manner and more so when she told me she had something to say.

"What's happened," I asked in a panic. "Did they take Marcos again? Did they call? Is that what it is?"

"No, no, calm down," she said. "Please sit down." And then came the news I never expected from such a good friend. We had been through so much together outside Brazil working for the UN. She said,

"It's that I just finished the application process to work for the First Secretary and . . ."

I interrupted her, guessing what it was: "You want me to leave, don't you."

"I can't risk my career right now!"

"But no one's coming after me. I'm not being persecuted by the police."

"But it is dangerous for me."

Without another word, I packed my bag and went to the home of my aunt. Before I left I wrote her a brief letter, which ended: "A friend in need is a friend indeed." I never saw her again.

While I was finishing my work in Brasília, Marcos visited the Apostolic Nuncio in Rio.* When I arrived in Rio and finally saw my son, our meeting was one of tears, joy, and happiness.

Despite our being reunited, I found Marcos to be very depressed. He moved into my apartment in Rio on Prudente de Morais Street, but it was a difficult time. Physically, Marcos seemed fine. He no longer limped, though the muscles on the right side of his face still trembled when he was upset. However, he would cry often, and for no apparent reason. He would go into his room and cry out of pity for those whom he had left behind. He refused

---

* *Editor's note.* The Apostolic Nuncio is a permanent diplomatic representative of the Vatican to a state or international organization.

to accept any special treatment, as if this would help those who were still suffering.

Técio recommended that Marcos not go outside alone so that he couldn't be kidnapped again without anyone knowing. And so I dedicated all of my time to him. From the moment Marcos arrived home, he never had another convulsion. In the meantime, he continued taking his medicine. We went to the beach every day, because it was good for him to exercise his left leg and his feet. We would walk and breathe in the fresh sea air, enjoying the ecstasy of freedom and our contact with nature. Little by little, his physical ailments disappeared. The psychological wounds took much longer.

I then began to try to convince Marcos that we should leave Brazil. At first he refused. He wanted to stay and work to help his country. So I asked him at least to submit his passport application as a test to see whether he would be allowed to leave, if by chance he wanted to. He initially resisted, but at last he gave in, and it turned out to be easy. Without any problem, they took his picture, he met with the necessary police officials, everything! This was a great relief to me.

I took him to meet the Consul General of the United States who had been so nice as to try and see Marcos in the hospital. The Consul immediately invited us to dinner. Marcos was depressed, though, and said little. He hardly ate and only commented on the waiter, "Look at this poor guy. He's exploited and has to work all day long." He later said, "How can I eat in this environment when there are so many others imprisoned eating only bread and water?" The Consul was very compassionate; he understood and said nothing. I was left to try to carry the conversation until the awkward meal had ended.

I began taking Marcos to see different doctors. I would go in first and tell the doctor what had happened to Marcos, and then I would leave so that the examination could be more comfortable for Marcos. The first neurologist we saw—I can't remember his name—paled when I described what had happened, and he said, "My dear woman, I've never treated any conditions resulting from torture! The only information about cases like this is in Germany, in the Nazi archives." He was shocked. He saw Marcos and prescribed some medicine for his convulsions and recommended he continue going to the beach to exercise his legs and feet.

I then went to another doctor, a famous specialist named Dr. Aaron Ackermann, who had been recommended to me by my brother-in-law. After explaining the situation and introducing Marcos, he said: "Don't ask me why nor how he had this convulsive reaction. Let's only talk about how we're going to cure him."

I was intrigued and a little perplexed by this statement. After performing an MRI, he said that Marcos was fine but that he should continue taking his medicine for some time. He didn't say anything about what might have happened to have caused nine months of tremors and convulsions. And so we left.

Around this time I decided to have a party for everyone who had helped in some way to free Marcos. For example, my ex-boss, who was then work-ing at the American Embassy, had leaked the information that the embassy had received a telegram from the State Department ordering them to help me in any way possible. I invited the Consul, our lawyers, and friends who had signed statements regarding Marcos's health. This was Marcos's first meeting with Técio, who was always so busy helping to save other people.

During the party, I noticed that Marcos seemed to monopolize Técio in a corner of the room. I went over at one point and said, "My son, why don't you go and talk with some of the others who also did so much for you?" He responded, "If you knew what Técio was telling me, you wouldn't complain so much." I left them and anxiously waited for the end of the party.

When the guests had left Marcos informed me, "Técio has learned from an inside source that they intend to arrest me again, because my file has been confused with that of a bank robber and terrorist. You know how long it will take to prove that I am innocent."

"Oh, my God! I won't let that happen."

We took a taxi and went directly to Técio's house. I asked him, "How long do we have to leave the country before this is going to happen?"

"Eight days," he responded.

The next day I ran to the Consul and asked for a visa for Marcos's pass-port, which was issued immediately. The Consul suggested that as soon as we reach Washington, D.C., we should meet with Immigration Services and have his visa changed from student to permanent status. We purchased our plane tickets, and four days later, May 8, 1971, we left for the airport. Nearly our entire family was there, along with many of our friends. We knew of cases where the police had entered the plane and arrested a passenger before takeoff, so we were all nervous and on edge as we waited. Finally, amid tears, hugs, and kisses, we boarded the plane, and I began praying that the flight would soon take off. Suddenly the plane was in the air!

My family said that, as the plane left the ground, everyone jumped for joy. Marcos was safe at last!

The next period of our lives is difficult to remember. I had left everything in Brazil—a furnished apartment in Rio, and all of my belongings—and I went to live with my daughter and her roommate in a house in Arlington, Virginia.

When I left for Rio the previous November, I had given up my apartment, along with everything I owned, and so I was left without a place to live in Washington. I also resigned my job with USAID. Upon returning to Washington, I not only had to reapply for work with the organization but also had to wait for a position to open. I was in a desperate financial situation.

Letter from Marcos to my mother:

May 10, 1971

It's now eleven o'clock at night, and a new day is fast approaching. I arrived here safely, and I'm now far from home and the dangers that were waiting for me there. Now, as you promised, it's time for me to relax and stop worrying about myself. I want to receive good news from you, since you're well and more peaceful. Did you see how beautiful the airport was, with so many of our friends there? It was very hard for me to leave you and everyone else. I felt such great friendship from everyone there waving goodbye as I walked up the stairs and disappeared into the plane. I know each person there believes in our fight, and that gives me joy. I still am just beginning to get settled here, but soon I'm going to encourage you to come here too.

Our flight was beautiful and serene. An enormous moon filled my window, and I slept uninterrupted until eight in the morning. I hardly felt anything. It was like a trip from Rio to São Paulo.

Marcos had already lived in the United States when he was a teenager. He had received a scholarship to study there and finished high school in Chicago. He had lived with a nice American family and made many friends.

Marcos's letter continued:

I got off the plane in New York, and it was as if I had never left. The flight was delightful. It was good to see Tiana [Cristiana's nickname—ed.]. She's beautiful with her black hair, and she's so skinny. She laughed the entire time. The house [in Virginia—ed.] is nice and well furnished, and the neighborhood is great. Both blacks and whites live here. (It's called an integrated neighborhood.) All of the streets are wide and lined with trees and grass, and the homes have large gardens, trees, flowers, tulips, azaleas, and dogwood. The green here is very soft and light, and, this, along with the Potomac River, fills me with peace and tranquility. It is such a contrast to the events of the past week when anti–Vietnam War demonstrators covered the streets and bridges, surrounded by police. It's also very different from the tropics with its disordered, alive, and aggressive natural beauty.

Washington is a beautiful city; I'm only now discovering how it's surrounded by nature. The leaf I've sent with this letter is from a maple tree, a beautiful tree with a light colored trunk that is tapped for sugar and delicious syrup. During the fall, these leaves turn the colors of dawn and fall dancing, by the thousands.

We are in the beginning of spring here, and everything is alive and flowering, just as I am. It's good for me to be happy and at peace. You are a wonderful person, dear to all of us. In the silence of the natural world, I thank God for me and for you. But the fight continues . . .

The days passed by, and Marcos read, slept, took walks. Father Colonnese organized a picnic one morning with several friends. When it was time to go, Marcos said that he wasn't going because he couldn't enjoy himself while others were suffering. I was very upset. My God, how can we be so rude to those who did so much to help us? After a long discussion, he gave in and ended up talking nearly the entire time with Father Colonnese.

As time went on, Marcos began to be invited to speak here and there, at a church or a university, to talk about what had happened to him and what was going on with the dictatorship in Brazil. He also put out a basket for people who wanted to help by donating money. There was a lot of curiosity, and, after his presentations, there were always many questions, and much sympathy.

While we were living near Washington, we were introduced to Pat and Liz French, who soon became dear friends.

Later Marcos recalled:

I remember we had been invited by Marge and Tom Melville to have lunch with them and another couple. It was toward the end of 1971.

Liz was a great fighter for the cause of justice and was constantly volunteering with various citizen groups in the United States.

She was a member of the Women's International League for Peace and Freedom that fought for Latin American causes. She also worked with a group that donated used clothing in good condition to migrant workers, etc. During the Vietnam War, she was arrested in front of the White House after lying down in the road in protest. The reason for her arrest was that she was trying to stop traffic. They called her "crime" "civil disobedience." She did not have to go to jail but received a warning.

Pat was an economist at the World Bank and felt a profound sense of solidarity with Liz's work in relation to the impoverished people of the Southern Hemisphere. Both spent five years in Ethiopia, just serving and doing good. From our first visit they became good friends. In the spring of 1972, when they learned that I couldn't afford the tuition for the Master's program in Economics at American University, they offered to pay it for me. Since then, having met my mother and some of my siblings, they have become "our family" in Bethesda, Maryland.

I would add that our gratitude for everything they did for us during this time is infinite. They have been true friends.

Letter from me to our family in Brazil:

May 12, 1971

We are dying to see you all, the beach, our apartment, and Rio . . .

Nevertheless, to be able to pass by a police car here and not be afraid, to think that Marcos can go where he wants without worrying if he's not home on time, to be able to sit at a restaurant and speak clearly about everything I'd like to without having to keep an eye out . . . it's worth every sacrifice.

Our flight here was very calm. Marcos said he hardly felt anything, which I do not doubt. You get a feeling of anesthesia when everything in your life is jumbled and crazy.

The weather was bad when we arrived in New York. It was rainy and cold. In D.C., there are blue skies, but it's very hot. Tiana and Sylvia cried when they met us. To my relief, we've only seen Marcos shake three times: once at seeing all of the flowers everywhere, then again in a music store, and last in the office of Father Colonnese, where there were posters in Spanish depicting a Brazilian general as a marionette puppet being controlled by an arm made up of the flags of the U.S., France, and England.

I hope Marcos is able to relax more here. His face still twitches at times, and he thinks it's a waste of time to watch TV or go for a walk, or just talk.

Letter from Marcos to Martinha:

December 27, 1971

. . . Did you watch President Médici's speech on TV? Or have you at least heard what happened? I found out that just before he began speaking at the OAS meeting, a Brazilian began yelling something. Everyone who was there saw it happen. Here it's been in all the papers, and there have been some other reports about some demonstrations in front of the White House that lasted for two days. They had posters with pictures simulating torture, and they also put on a play that was very well done. It really had an impact on a lot of people in a serious way.

In New York, they presented a film on TV made by an American about the 70 Brazilians who were exiled in Chile, and there was a panel of specialists discussing the current situation in our country.*

We found out in the fall of 1971 that an official meeting was scheduled to take place at the White House between President Médici and President Nixon in December. So a group of us, including an American couple from CARIB (the Committee Against Repression in Brazil), and a theatre group called Earth Onion decided to plan our own reception. Marcos helped to prepare everything as well, but thought it best not to be directly involved.

---

* *Editor's note*. This film was *Brazil: A Report on Torture*. It was made by Saul Landau and Haskell Wexler in 1971. In the documentary, the filmmakers interviewed some of the seventy political prisoners that were released in January 1971 and flown to Chile in exchange for the freedom of the Swiss ambassador who had been kidnapped by a revolutionary organization known as Vanguarda Popular Revolucionária. In the film, the former torture victims reenact the techniques used on them while they were in prison.

We took pictures of him simulating the different techniques used by the torturers of political prisoners, and we used these photographs in the demonstration we organized.

We chose Lafayette Square, which is right in front of the White House. We brought posters with information, diagrams, and pictures denouncing the Brazilian dictatorship. We included information regarding political prisoners and prepared an enormous banner that read: "Stop U.S. Dollar Complicity with Brazilian Torture." At the time, we knew that the U.S. had not only helped to finance and aid the military coup of 1964 but was continuing to transfer millions of public dollars in aid to the Brazilian dictatorship.

The first morning of the demonstration it was raining a little. Because of this, President Médici did not enter through the rear garden entrance but was brought in a limousine to the front of the White House near the park. This change gave the four of us (Augusto [Meyer—ed.] and I, and the American couple) enough time to move in front of the limousine where we stood, our mouths gagged with small Brazilian flags. After they entered we returned to the park. As part of the initial greetings, they all had to wait outside while both national anthems were played. From where they were standing, they had a clear view of our banner and protest demonstration. Members of the press photographed the entire scene. Soon thereafter, White House staff brought out huge green partitions to block their view of us.

We had decided to stage the demonstration during the lunch hour because many people often eat in the park. Because of the weather, we were unable to talk to many of them, as most were in a hurry to get out of the rain. It was also quite cold, and we left early to get something warm to eat.

Success came the next day. It was beautiful and sunny. We hung pictures and flyers about the dictatorship on a line strung through the park. We played Brazilian music and distributed informational leaflets to passersby. Soon, two limousines with tinted windows drove up and parked between us and the White House. I could see that from the inside of the vehicle someone was taking pictures of us. I don't know if they were from the CIA or the FBI, but they were all wearing dark suits and hats. I went up to them and offered them a pamphlet, but they didn't take one.

After a while I sat down to rest for a moment, and a man approached me. He wore an anguished expression and exclaimed, "But this is exactly what the Nazis did! I'm a Jew who survived the concentration camps." And he showed me the number tattooed on his arm. We spoke for a little while, and he wished us the best of luck.

Suddenly a young man ran up and said, "I just shouted, 'Down with the Dictatorship' in the OAS meeting."

"What?" I asked and called for the others to come over.

The young man explained that he was able to get a press pass and gain entrance to the public seating area of the OAS meeting. Just as President Médici was beginning to speak, he stood up and yelled, "Down with the Dictatorship." He was immediately taken by security and removed from the room. When they saw he was unarmed, they sent him away. This young Brazilian, whose name was Peter Kami, had lived in the United States for a while and had even developed a little bit of an accent, and he was quite courageous to do what he did. He became a good friend, and we had him over for a typical Brazilian meal of rice and beans, which he said he missed.

At noon on the second day, the play began. One young woman was dressed in a military uniform, with a green field coat and a general's hat. Another wore a Nixon mask, a suit coat, and a top hat with dollar bills taped to it. "Nixon" sat in a chair and said to the "general," "Come on, come sit in my lap."

The general came and sat, and Nixon asked him, "What have you done for us there in your country?"

The general took out a wad of contracts from his wallet.

"Ah, very good! And what have you done with the subversives?"

The general held his arm like a machine-gun and said, "Tataratatata"

"Excellent," responded the American.

As this was going on, another woman laid in the grass off to the side. Her body was connected to several electric wires, and her mouth was gagged. She cried out in pain.

I couldn't watch this scene any longer and left. "I can't take this," I told the others. I didn't see the end of the play; I only know that when it was over everyone turned to the White House and yelled with their fists in the air, "The People United Will Never Be Defeated!"

That night there was a cocktail party at the Brazilian Embassy.

The next day an article in the *Washington Post* stated there had never been as much security for a visiting head of state as for the president of Brazil.

Chapter Sixteen

An armed soldier was posted on nearly every corner of the city—what an embarrassment!

Shortly thereafter we were told by our family in Rio that my mother had grown very thin and frail. She went to see several doctors, but they couldn't find anything wrong with her. I went to Rio to visit her and was shocked and even afraid to see how thin she was. The doctors finally concluded that her condition was the result of everything that had happened, all of the afflictions and fears she had developed, along with seeing her grandson in such poor health. They advised her to forget what had happened. We all reacted against this—we must never forget!

Thankfully, mother returned to normal after a few months.

Letter from my mother to me:

September 9, 1971

. . . Tiana says Marcos has already started at the university and that he had gone to his first class when I called. I was very happy to hear this. If he stays with it, he may find he likes it; and, it could be a good career for him.

To Marcos she wrote:

The only thing I beg of you, Marcos, is that you don't try to return to Brazil.

In the beginning, it was hard for Marcos to study. He would read and try to study, but within fifteen minutes he would fall asleep. It was so difficult for him to concentrate. One day he slammed his fist on the table and said through his tears, "They destroyed me, Mom, I can't even study anything!"

I responded, "Be patient son, you've been away from everything for so long, hospitalized and living in terror. You have to train your mind again, little by little, in order to return to what you were before. When your leg was paralyzed, didn't you have to exercise it before it returned to normal? So now you have to do some mental exercises in order to be able to study and remember everything."

With great effort and force of will, Marcos continued with his education and completed a master's degree in Economics at American University in Washington, D.C.

Letter from my mother to me:

Rio de Janeiro, October 9, 1971

. . . After so many days of waiting, Martinha came over yesterday to tell me that a decision was finally made by the military court about Marcos's case. She says it was a joke! The prosecutor had nothing to accuse Marcos of; he had no proof that Marcos was subversive. The discussion in the court was drawn out, and they nearly declared him not guilty. They had included his case with one against an organization called REDE [Resistência Democrática (Democratic Resistance)—ed.] that they considered to be terrorist. The DOPS agents who forced Marcos to give a confession in the hospital included his statement in the case against REDE. Técio proved in court that it was all a lie, that he had always been innocent, that they had mistreated him, and then looked for an excuse to charge him. He emphasized that Marcos was the son of an American citizen and that this made the situation more serious, especially because his mother worked for the State Department. The whole matter could create diplomatic problems. He repeated again that Marcos was innocent and that he had never belonged to any subversive group, violent or not.

Martinha says that no one moved while Técio spoke. They just listened without interruption, and, at the end, they unanimously acquitted Marcos. What a relief! Marcos, you can raise your head up again, but stay where you are, because they could still re-arrest you.

While this was going on, we were doing everything we could to obtain a permanent visa for Marcos. This in and of itself was another odyssey. I wrote my mother the following letter:

Washington, D.C., November 7, 1971

. . . The other thing that has taken all of my time has been resolving the issue of Marcos's visa. I was at last able to speak with the man who is substituting for the man who initiated our request in the office of Mike Colonnese, who's on vacation. He was very efficient and not bureaucratic. He told us that Marcos could begin working. He also told us about a law, which was not very well known, that prohibited the U.S. government from deporting anyone who felt physically threatened in their country of origin.

If Marcos were caught working, which was highly unlikely, he would have to go to an immigration office and swear that he could not go back to Brazil. This would resolve everything. The person who gave us this information assured us that it was accurate. I was very relieved. Marcos immediately applied for a Social Security card and began to look for a job. He has already filled out several applications and is just waiting to hear back. He's also going to visit an employment agency that is related to the field of geology, his former profession.

We are continuing to fight and tell the world what Brazil is doing to its political prisoners. For example, Marcos was recently interviewed by the *Washington Post*.* The story took up an entire page and included an enormous "close-up" shot. He said he doesn't believe that President Médici isn't aware of torture. The practice has become routine and has now victimized more than ten thousand people. He said the country's apparent economic success is hollow because the great majority of people continue to live in poverty. Have you heard of the economic theory adopted by Roberto Campos and Delfim Netto that you should make the rich richer so that their wealth will overflow to the poor? It's the same as Nixon's "trickledown" theory that's causing so many problems here.†

It was not Marcos who explained all of this to me, but my American friends, professors, and government officials who are horrified by what is happening in Brazil. They are becoming more and more interested and involved in Marcos's case. You probably haven't seen this. You live under a regime of terror and my dream is to see the entire family out of the country, but they are complacent or too afraid.

We recently met with an important person in the State Department who said, "You have no idea what a 'revolution' you caused here in this country and in the State Department. You cannot calculate the degree and proportion of your influence as a result of your actions to save your son."

We all believe that, because of the power of the press, if they were to touch anyone in the family in Brazil, they would be made to suffer intense public opposition throughout the world. Marcos's article in the *Washington Post* provoked an enormous public reaction. Hundreds of people wrote letters to the *Washington Post*, [and] to the Brazilian Embassy denouncing the torture, and to the United States Congress calling for the end of economic aid to Brazil. Can you see how much we've done? Can you see how much we've even influenced the inter-

---

* *Editor's note.* Dan Griffin, "The Torture of a Brazilian," *Washington Post* (September 19, 1971): D 31. As a result of this article, the *Washington Post* published an editorial denouncing torture in Brazil. "Brazil and Torture," *Washington Post* (September 16, 1971): E-6.

† *Editor's note.* Roberto de Oliveira Campos was the Brazilian Minister of Planning from 1964 to 1967. Antonio Delfim Netto was Minister of Finance from 1967 to 1974, and later Minister of Agriculture and Minister of Planning. Both economists were pro-business and favored large-scale foreign investment, which many critics of the military regime argued widened the gap between the rich and the poor.

national aid policy of their congress? I think it's essential that they educate the public...

Why do you think Médici came here? To ask for money, more money...

Don't give up, my dear mother, and don't think the things you said in your letter, "nothing changes, nor do men." If that were so, there would never have been any historic changes, such as the independence of countries, the French Revolution, the creation of the labor unions, the Russian and Chinese revolutions, etc.

Millions are fighting for peace while all of this is happening. Today we are fighting an economic war. It's those with money and the dictatorship against those who believe in a more equitable distribution of wealth and a better lifestyle for everyone. (I believe [a better world— ed.] is possible if we had truly democratic elections.) The churches are with us. I cannot sit, be apathetic, and just watch what is going on without participating in it. They say here that in the world there only two types of people: the doers and the watchers. Marcos and I are among those who are doing something.

Letter from Marcos to Martinha:

June 3, 1971

You can only imagine how hard it is for me, how much I miss you all. I left so much, so many dear people, and for such an indeterminate amount of time. I'm faced with a situation that's completely new, and there's so much for me to do and overcome. But therein hides the riches of this new stage of my life. I have been able to choose options that have always meant a challenge, a constant rebirth . . .

Mike [Colonnese—ed.] arrived three days ago, and for three days I have been working with him on something of great importance. Mike is someone who is so frank, direct, transparent, and sensitive that, after three days, it's as if we are already old friends. He is a rare person, truly unconcerned with personal gain and interested only in service to people here and in every corner of the world. That is why he is loved and respected in so many countries, persecuted by groups in others, and prevented from entering still others.

To our regret, Mike Colonnese was removed from his position as director of the Latin American division of the U.S. Catholic Conference. Mike told the *Washington Post* in an articled dated September 7, 1971, "My ideology was too advanced for the U.S. Catholic Conference."

It still remained hard for Marcos to deal with the fact that his political friends were so far away. This was especially the case after seeing the film, *Brazil: A Report on Torture.*

Letter from Marcos to Martinha:

Washington, D.C., July 13, 1971

Today my spirits are very low and hurt, for I've just seen the film about the people in Chile. I saw my old friend Neném, and in the film he spoke about me with such feeling that I became emotional. It's all so sad and so far from over that I feel like I could cry at any moment. I don't know how I'm going to be able to release all of this energy that's building up within me.

But I've been well. Our work is growing in size and importance. I feel like I'm returning to normal, and, little by little, my creative capacities are returning.

Letter from Marcos to Martinha:

Washington, D.C., July 17, 1971

I made a quick trip to Europe with some good results. I saw several wonderful things and felt again the warmth of friendship from some old friends.

Here, life goes on and little by little is becoming more concrete and purposeful.

It's not easy to be alone in such a large country as this, but I'm meeting good people and things are improving for me.

Letter from Marcos to Martinha:

Quebec, September 20, 1971

God bless you! Mom just telephoned me to say that I was acquitted and that you are all happy there.

I owe so much to you and to everyone there for everything you've done for me. It may seem as though we're far away and somewhat disconnected from you, but it's not true. I'm able to imagine all of the effort, worry, hope, and cost of what you have done for me, and my gratitude is infinite. You know how much I would like to be there with you in our beloved country, but for my own good and for all of our peace of mind, I'm here far from you. I'm trying to explore every opportunity so as to be more useful in the future and by taking advantage of the rich experiences life offers me. Give everyone there a big hug from me.

With Mike's departure from the Latin American Bureau, my work ended there and I decided to come to Quebec. All of my friends were eager to help finance my trip here, as well as to the other places I've been.

Try to imagine, if you can, my frustration when we arrived at the Canadian border at 11:30 at night, and they wouldn't let me enter. It wasn't anything serious, and in fact it was ridiculous. The border officer was an old and ill-humored civil servant who asked me a thousand questions about the purpose of my trip, how long I was going to stay there, where I was living in the United States, etc. Finally he asked me if I had purchased a return trip to the United States. I told him that I tried to buy one, but the bus company suggested that, since I was going to go to California from Quebec, I might as well buy my ticket there. He asked if I had purchased a return ticket to Brazil. I told him no, and because I was upset, I unwisely told him that I was thinking of becoming a resident of the United States.

Immediately, the old grump said that I couldn't enter Canada because my intentions invalidated my status as a simple tourist. I was very upset and because I couldn't understand his reasoning, I strongly protested without success.

Back in New York, I telephoned my friends there, and they explained to me that Canada has a serious problem with unemployment. They do everything they can to prevent immigrants from entering.

I took another bus and went to Buffalo, instead of Montreal, and on to Niagara Falls and Toronto. Everything went well, and I arrived, without further problems, in Quebec. There are some wonderful and dedicated people here who are working intensely for Brazil through the Comitê Solidarité Brésil. I attended a fascinating conference on Latin America sponsored by the Centre Quebecois de Relations Internationales.

Letter from Marcos to Martinha:

Washington, D.C., October 21, 1971

I'm still in the middle of that damned fight to try to obtain the famous green card. They have required a thousand things (such as receiving a job offer as a geologist), and I can hardly stand the wait and the bureaucracy. They now want my certificate from the geology program along with all of the materials and grades from each of the courses I took. The urgency for this is extreme because they want it by the end of October at the latest!

I'm still working a lot. The people at the Latin American Bureau have been quite passive in terms of helping me. It seems they've adopted the policy of "letting things go." I am applying for a scholarship that could finance my master's degree and allow me to study what interests me, but it's not easy.

As for my health, I admit that some of Mom's worrying is legitimate. I'm taking some new medicine that the doctor prescribed. At first, I was taking large doses, following the doctor's orders, of three pills a day, but this made me so tired that I've lowered it to two. Now I'm feeling much better. My next appointment is being moved up in view of the trips I'll be taking at the end of November.

Letter from Marcos to my mother:

December 30, 1971

I've begun to participate in group therapy at the Georgetown Hospital for an hour and a half a week at $2 a session, until I have a regular job. I'm also going to have an appointment with a neurologist at the beginning of January. I've tried not to depend on anyone financially. Sometimes Mom gives me money, but the truth is that, since I began working at the Latin American Bureau of the United States Conference of Catholic Bishops, I've become almost financially independent. I've been working as a writer and researcher, for which they pay me, and I've also given several talks, which are paid as well.

I'm going to the West Coast in February as part of my work, and as soon as my visa issue is resolved, I'll decide on which program to apply for at the university. I won't start a doctoral program until the spring or later, but, in the meantime, I will probably do economic research for the Latin American Bureau.

I'm not so worried about losing time as I was before. I've tried to relax and reacquire my old, solid methods. I've also tried to do fewer things, but better. This is very important.

This is how we spent the first year following Marcos's release, but we still had to fight to survive financially and to obtain Marcos's permanent visa.

I was working and traveling nonstop, thanks to the help of my "bosses," as we called the people who contracted "freelance" translators like me. They knew of our situation and always gave me small groups to interpret for so that I could work longer and make more money. We were still living in the home of my daughter and her friend. They were covering many of our expenses, and it was an embarrassing situation for us.

Letter from me to Senator Ted Kennedy:

Washington, D.C., 1972
Esteemed Senator Kennedy,

I am sending the enclosed documents to try and help you understand what my son and my family have been going through for the past year in Brazil and now here.

After all the fighting, tears, humiliation, and pain, my son Marcos was freed on February 1, 1971, and in May we were able to flee Brazil.

During this time we have been greatly helped and supported by the U.S. Catholic Conference, Latin American Bureau. Nevertheless, there is not much they can do regarding the difficulty of obtaining a visa that will allow us to stay in the U.S.

We have been told that Marcos must receive a contract offer of employment in order to obtain a resident visa that will allow him to work. Even then, the application process would require fourteen to sixteen months.

I know that you are the Chair of the Senate Subcommittee on Exiles, and, for this reason, I am asking for your help.

How can a thirty-year-old man recover from the horrible cruelty he suffered as a political prisoner if he is not given permission to work for the next two years, or who knows how long?

I have been informed that the fact that I am an American citizen has no bearing on this case, because my son is more than twenty-one years old. To me this seems unjust.

For this reason, I am pleading for your help and interest. I know that senators can make accommodations for individuals to receive permanent resident visas in special cases. Would you do this for us?

If you need more information, we can be contacted at the following address . . .

Marcos still requires some medical assistance, but he is capable of working. It is very humiliating for a man of his age to depend on others for the smallest expense.

I am certain that you will compassionately understand our purpose, which is much more psychological in nature than economic.

Therefore, I wish to thank you for your cooperation and attention and express our gratitude in every way possible.

Sincerely,

Lina

To this letter I attached all of the documents and letters that related to Marcos's situation. Despite this, I was greatly disappointed that we never received even the shortest letter or telephone call in response!

We spent another Christmas far from our loved ones in Rio.

We continued to collect every article or news item that was published about Brazil, the political prisoners held by the government, and the continued use of torture.

My mother wrote Marcos in one of her letters: "You should have read in the *Jornal do Brasil* about the fact that they absolved you for the second time in a court in São Paulo. But, regardless, you cannot return, because your speeches, interviews, and letters have had an impact here."

Técio wrote to us soon after:

Rio, June 6, 1972

Dear Lina:,

I'm sending you the final result of our work. Marcos's appeal has been heard in court, and he was unanimously acquitted! Mission accomplished!

I am including the official publications . . .

It's been months and months since I have seen anyone from the family here in Rio. And I haven't heard any news from your end.

Give Marcos a hug for me and tell him to write.

Love,

Técio

Técio's letter brought us such great relief. We celebrated with wine, but, in our hearts, there was still the sadness over the impossibility of returning to Brazil. In reality, I didn't want to go back as long as the dictatorship was in power, but my children did not share this vision. As much as I pleaded, "Come here. You'll have more opportunities here than you have there, and you'll be free from fear and repression," they refused.

Our fight to obtain a resident visa continued. Marcos wrote a letter to Immigration Services:

Washington, D.C., May 17, 1972
Mr. Sewell
Immigration and Naturalization Service
United States Department of Justice
Dear Sir,

I have been asked to write a statement explaining, in detail, why I believe I would be persecuted if I were to return to my country of origin. After carefully considering how to present my case as clearly as possible and after examining the many documents I have in my possession, I have decided that the documents I am including with this letter should be more than sufficient to prove what I allege. I have many other documents to present you regarding the current situation in Brazil and the treatment given to those who in any way demonstrate their opposition, be it by ideas or acts, regarding the authoritarian regime that is controlling our country and has imposed itself on the citizens of Brazil since 1964. But I decided to choose those documents that best express my ordeal and that justify my hope that I will by accepted into this country, where, based on its democratic traditions, there is dialogue and the right to an opinion. Here people can fight for the rights of equality and opportunity.

These are the three precious values of my life. One could even say they are the foundation of my thoughts and ideals.

The first documents relate the correspondence that my mother and I have sent to the Holy Father. They represent proof so strong that they merited publication in the Congressional Record.* The second

* U.S. Congress. Senate. Subcommittee of the Committee on Appropriations. *Hearings on Foreign Assistance and Related Programs,* 93rd Congress, 1st session. January 25, 1972 (Washington, D.C.: Government Printing Office, 1972), 1374–76.

is an interview I gave to the *Washington Post*, in September 1971, and the last is a very recent article about the barbarous treatment inflicted on those who have been indiscriminately imprisoned. This article also contains the ... the testimony of the woman who wrote a letter [about how I had been tortured] and who I saw for the last time on the occasion described by her.

I would like to add that there have been many instances in which people who have courageously and honestly spoken the truth about torture suffered at the hands of the Brazilian military and police and who have asked for international help in order to bring an end to such atrocities, have been imprisoned again, persecuted, mistreated, and even killed upon returning to my beloved and long-suffering country.

I am currently receiving medical treatment, and I have to recover completely so that I can become a good and productive citizen. I am certain that in Brazil I will not find conditions suitable for this, and I fear that I will not be able to stay alive in my country. For this reason, I pray for your comprehension and human solidarity. My mother, who is an American citizen, guarantees that in no circumstances will I become a burden on this country.

Sincerely,

Marcos Arruda

Marcos continued doing political work about the situation in Brazil that included a trip to Mexico. This alarmed my mother.

Letter from my mother to me:

Rio, July 9, 1972

I have just received a postcard from Marcos in Mexico. He loves it there and has even asked me to send him some books. But I ask myself, with a student visa, will he lose his status as a political refugee? I am truly afraid that he will give in to the crazy idea of coming back. This would do me in. Everything is the same here. We hear all the time of people who have become "sick and hospitalized."

With my work I was constantly traveling to New York with small groups of visiting dignitaries. One day, I received a phone call at my home in Washington from an old friend, Zuzu Angel, an internationally known fashion designer. She asked me to meet her at the Gotham Hotel, where she was staying, the next time I was in New York. And so I did.

We had a long conversation, and she wanted to know what I had done to be able to get Marcos released from jail. She said that, in her case, all of her efforts to help her son, who had also been arrested by the political police, had been in vain, including letters from his American father and requests by influential people. I told her in detail what I had done, though I had heard that her son might have already been killed. They said that one of his cellmates had watched through the bars of a high window as he was taken from the prison and then dragged behind a jeep with his mouth tied to the exhaust pipe. They say the driver was Brigadier Burnier. Poor Zuzu! What an inconsolable horror!

I finally got up my courage and said to her, "Zuzu, why can't you accept the possibility that he is already dead? If you haven't been allowed to see him, and no one has received any word from him, what do you have to hope for?

She responded, "I will only believe that he is dead when I see his body. I will not accept any lies or hypotheses."

Unfortunately, we never saw each other again. I received a single letter from her, but my gypsy lifestyle took me far away, and I only learned later what had happened in New York.

To raise public awareness about her son and the political situation in Brazil, Zuzu organized a fashion show at the Brazilian Consulate. One of the models who participated was a daughter of Mayor John Lindsey. Zuzu dressed herself all in black, with a veil over her face and an enormous silver chain around her neck from which hung a large silver angel. In the middle of the show, her daughter, who plays the guitar, sang a song for her missing brother. All of the upper crust of New York City was present, since Zuzu made clothes for all of them. Some of her fashion designs were embroidered with images of birds trapped in cages, general's hats, rifles, and tanks.

This political fashion show was a great success and had significant repercussions in the newspapers and on TV. In fact, it was from watching television that I learned about it. I was so happy for Zuzu and thought, "That's the way, my courageous Zuzu, give it to them . . ."

I later learned that when Henry Kissinger came to Brazil, Zuzu managed to get past security and sat waiting for him in a hotel corridor until she could give him a file about the imprisonment and torture of her son Stuart.

I greatly admire and respect the battle Zuzu fought, and I lament being unable to help her further. I later learned about the suspicious circumstances of her death in 1976, which many thought had been an assassination. Considering how outspoken she was, it is entirely possible.

I hope you are with your son now, Zuzu, at rest and at peace.

We had to fight not just to obtain a green card, but also to renew Marcos's passport when it expired. The press of several countries continued to publish our story, and it was even featured in books such as *Hidden Terrors*, written by A. J. Langguth, about the U.S. government's support of the Brazilian police. In one section of the book about Dan Mitrione, who had been sent to Brazil to "advise" the police, Langguth wrote:

> When a team of undergraduate scientists journeyed up from Rio to Minas Gerais, Dan Mitrione was already deep in his efforts to improve the Belo Horizonte police. The students composed another sort of advisory mission: they wanted to find ways to make the state's iron-ore deposits, the largest in the world, turn a healthier profit for Brazil.
>
> One team member was a small, round-faced, wavy-haired student named Marcos Arruda. Enrolled in the school of geology at the University of Rio de Janeiro, Marcos did not look like either a revolutionary or a martyr; and certainly during the years of the Goulart regime, his questioning of Brazil's social order was tentative and very respectful.*

In his book, Langguth describes in detail Marcos's ordeal in a chapter entitled "The Truth about U.S. Police Operation in Latin America."

Marcos commented in a letter to my mother dated November 3, 1978:

> The author of the book *Hidden Terrors* interviewed me several times over a period of three years. All of my work to denounce the torture and oppression of our people while I have been in the United States has been in reference to the period of President Médici. The last public

* A. J. Langguth, *Hidden Terrors* (New York: Pantheon Books, 1978), 80.

statement I made was on a national television program in 1974, when I said that Brazilians had hopes that General Geisel, in contrast to the other presidents, would fulfill his promises of restoring democracy to the country and ending torture and arbitrary imprisonment.

Regarding the two lists from the embassies in Brazil and in Washington that contain my name, one dates from 1973 and the other from 1975.

I had been informed by a friend who worked at the embassy that the appearance of Marcos's name on these lists meant Marcos could be killed even in the airport upon arrival for having spoken out against Brazil from outside the country.

The letter continued:

Yesterday I met with a friend who had just returned from there [Brazil] who suggested that it would be much better for me to fly into Viracopos than Rio, since the repressive system had become almost autonomous and had been dismantled there following the scandal of the assassination of Vladimir Herzog and Manuel Fiel Filho.

At this time we had been considering allowing Marcos to visit Brazil, but a lot of water passed under the bridge before this was possible.

On February 19, 1974, Marcos wrote from Washington to the reverend William Wipfler of the Latin American Working Group of the National Counsel of Churches in New York City:

As you know, I cannot return to Brazil without risking my life. I have been in the United States, first as a tourist and then as a student, for around three years already. Since I have a Brazilian passport, it would be foolish to think of asking for political asylum, because I would automatically lose both my citizenship and my passport, and I would not be allowed to leave this country and return to Brazil. Thus, the best way to resolve my problem, since my mother is also an American citizen, is to try to obtain an immigration visa for myself.

The first time I applied for this [a permanent resident visa] as a geologist but was refused because "they are not in need of geologists." With the help of a lawyer, I am currently exploring other options.

They are three:

1) Have a senator introduce legislation requesting that I be given a visa. (My lawyer says that this is approved 40% of the time.) If this is done, I automatically lose my student visa and remain in limbo until the legislation is voted on. If, at that point, it is approved then I must immediately leave the country to receive the visa at any American Consulate.
2) Marry an American. Besides involving many problems, it's risky.
3) Receive an offer of work that convincingly shows that I am someone highly qualified and specialized to fill the position at the institution making the offer. We have already spoken about this, and I think that this is the opportune moment. Could you explore the possibility of the Latin American Working Group or even of the National Counsel of Churches sending the required paperwork asking for a permanent resident visa for me, explaining that you need someone specialized in Latin America?

Letter from the law firm of David, Carliner, and Gordon to Marcos:

September 7, 1976

Your principal occupation seems to be that of an economist and will not be considered as essential in this country by the Employment and Training Administration, which approves the certification of foreigners seeking employment here. Nevertheless, since your specialization is Latin American Development, and you also are qualified to be a geologist, it might be possible to receive a job offer that combines these experiences, which will then allow you to obtain the certificate of employment for foreigners . . .

Meanwhile, since you already have an F-1 student visa, you can enter and leave the country as long as you are enrolled in a Ph.D. program.

Letter from my mother to me:

May 11, 1976

I no longer hope that you will return to live in Brazil. Life here is becoming absurd. I was hopeful at the beginning of this government, but now I no longer am . . .

Chapter Twenty

After all the energy that was spent to dismiss the commander of the Second Army because of the death of that journalist and the closing of the OBAN, which today is the DOI [Departamento de Operações Internas do Exercito (Department of Internal Operations of the Army)—ed.], everyone thought things were going to get better; but, all of a sudden, there have been so many imprisoned, etc., that we are very depressed.

And the battle continued . . .

Marcos studied various possibilities of how to renew his Brazilian passport and considered writing to Brazil to ask Técio to help him. He had several friends who had sent their passports to Geneva, but after six months had still heard nothing. Marcos even thought about trying to become a citizen of Guinea-Bissau, or asking for asylum from Switzerland, where he had lived and worked, or asking for asylum here in the United States. There was even the remote possibility that he could receive Italian citizenship by claiming to be the great-grandson of an Italian by the name of Sattamini.

Finally, after much travail, Marcos received the following letter:

The United States Senate, January 3, 1977
Dear Mr. Arruda:

Since our office last corresponded with you in February, 1976, about your immigration problems, there has been a change in the Immigration Laws.

On January 1, 1977, a new immigration law went into effect that eliminates the exclusion of people from the Western Hemisphere from the preference system. Under the preference system, all visas subject to quota are first issued to unmarried sons or daughters of U.S. citizens. There is no requirement that unmarried children be under the age of 21.

If you still desire to become a permanent resident, I suggest that you file an application with the Consulate in Switzerland with a notation that you now qualify for a first preference immigration visa.

Our office will do anything we can to help expedite the process once the application is filed.
Sincerely,

Linda Jacobson
Assistant Counsel

During the long years of waiting, praying, and constant effort trying to change Marcos's situation to one of greater security and stability, nothing pleased us more or made us happier than the wonderful news of this change in immigration law! God was surely with us!

Marcos submitted the appropriate application, and on April 26, 1977, I received the following memorandum from Immigration Services:

> Your petition to classify status of an alien relative for issuance of an immigrant visa has been received.
>
> This office is experiencing delays in processing all applications promptly. To avoid an additional delay in processing your application, please do not telephone or write to inquire about your application while your case is pending.
>
> If, however, you change your address, please notify this office by mail, referring to the above file number.
>
> Very truly yours,
> Joseph A. Mongiello
> District Director

Letter from Marcos to me:

Geneva, April 22, 1977

. . . I wanted to update you about the situation with my passport. I took it to the consulate together with all of the required documents (my enlistment information, voter's card, identity) and photos. I filled out the required forms, and they told me I should return on the 22nd to receive my passport. This happened on the 18th. I went there, and my passport was still there and hadn't been renewed! I asked why, and they said I should talk with the Consul. I waited for two hours until he got out of a meeting. Finally, I spoke with him. I was very polite, and he gave me a written statement that the passport is at the consulate being renewed (I need this document to show the Immigration Police, known as the Contrôle de l'Habitant), and he also told me that they needed to consult with Brasília by telegram since my passport has already been renewed once. But he thinks that within "three to four weeks" I will have an answer.

Now, this is in fact a very long time to wait, but I'll wait. Nevertheless, it's clear that the reason for consulting Brasília is a question of security. Therefore, it's now all in the hands of the National Intelligence Service . . .

Letter from Marcos to my mother:

April 5, 1977

You were right!

You better sit down before reading this. This morning I went to the consulate to receive my already renewed passport! I thanked the person who gave it to me, and now we are set until 1979. Wow! It is really incredible how they have continued to persecute us abroad. A few years ago there was a list of names at the embassies that was two pages long. Today, that list takes up five books! Can you believe it?

They say that the country is in incredible chaos. Something must happen soon. Can you imagine that fifty-six colonels signed a document saying that there is no longer any subversion in the country, but rather an authentic desire for democracy and that democratization is the only way to overcome the crises that are growing, etc.? They are an anti-communist group from Vila Militar [Military Academy—ed.], but they are also sick of the current totalitarianism and the insufferable crises that plague the country. . . . But, this is also being discussed in closed circles even as General Silvio Frota, Armando Falcão, and others demand that the government take away the political rights of sixty congressmen. And, in the meantime, the death squadrons continue to kill and get away with it.

Letter from Marcos to my mother:

November 19, 1978

I decided to put off my trip to Brazil until the end of January, when I will have finished my work in Africa. It seems that this coincides with Técio's opinion that I should not go in December. I've planned with Mother to go to the United States on December 16, and I'll stay there for Christmas. She's going from there to Rio at the beginning of the year. I will go from Dakar around January 25, and I'll stay until February 17.

This should give you enough time to prepare the papers so that I can renew my passport. I believe Técio or one of his assistants can take care of this.

As the time for Marcos's first return to Brazil drew close, we were very worried. We had heard several stories about people who were killed shortly after arrival, or who were imprisoned again, etc. But Técio's counsel was good enough for us, and if he said that Marcos could come, then we would agree.

Finally, the great day arrived! Marcos was working as an economic advisor to the World Council of Churches. Many other exiles had already returned, and now it was our turn. Besides all of the preparations we made in terms of food and getting the house ready, we made other plans with Marcos via letters. For example, we planned for him to wear a bright red shirt so that the flight attendants could more easily remember his appearance or at least remember the color. When he arrived in Rio, he told the flight attendants that he had family waiting for him and that, if he should be detained, would they please inform them.

Everything went as planned, and there were about eighty of us waiting for him at the Galeão Airport. Técio had recommended that, for Marcos's sake, we should not give any interviews. There were many reporters present, as well as a group of women who were mothers of exiles. The press asked many questions, and I kept my responses to a minimum, although I was dying to open my mouth and tell the whole story! I thanked the press for their cooperation over the years and only said that Marcos had come for a holiday and was staying a short time.

The attorney Modesto da Silveira, who later became a congressman, was there and was able to enter the immigration and customs area to wait for Marcos in person. What a relief!

When I saw the flight attendants leaving, I asked them about Marcos, and one of them said that he had been detained, but that he was there with an attorney.

From outside the windows of the immigration area we could see Modesto walking back and forth with his arm on the back of an Immigration official, trying to convince him that Marcos was innocent, that he had not seen his family in eight years, that he was going straight home, and that if they wanted to interrogate him they could set up an appointment. He would take Marcos there in person wherever they liked. All of this lasted for three long and agonizing hours.

The airport was completely under police control. They held Marcos in an isolated room and asked him a thousand questions and even threatened him. They went through his bags meticulously, saying that he could be a "carrier pigeon of subversion from abroad." They confiscated books, slides, and even records that he had brought for the family.

Then, after all of our waiting, he finally came out and into our happy arms.

The press did not understand Técio's request that we not give any interviews or make any detailed statements at that moment in order to avoid persecution while Marcos was in Brazil. Accordingly, we were criticized in the papers the next day.

After leaving the airport, I went with Marcos and my son-in-law to meet with Técio. Técio immediately asked:

"Marcos, did you come to denounce the government or to really spend some time with your family?"

"No, I came to be with my family and rest."

"Excellent," Técio said. "Now, you just need to follow my advice. Never go out alone. Avoid any contact with people considered suspicious 'by them,' and don't leave Rio. Everything should go well."

And so it did. I spent most of my time accompanying Marcos: at the beach, on the street, when he visited anyone, and during one of his interrogations. Marcos described his first interrogation, which occurred soon after he arrived. He went with his father and with Modesto da Silveira. I can't describe what happened, but I remember the comments Marcos made afterwards: "That man is an uneducated imbecile. He asked me details of my life since I had left Brazil. Things like:

"What newspapers did you read in the United States?"

"The *Washington Post*, *Le Monde*, etc."

And the interrogator responded, furious, "How can you read *Le Monde* in the United States if it is a French paper?"

And Marcos responded, "They import foreign papers."

This was too much.

The second time he was interrogated was in the Praça Mauá, in the pink building of the Federal Police building.

We waited for a little while, and then Marcos entered a room. They left the door open. I waited outside, but I could see that Marcos and the interrogator sat facing each other with their legs crossed.

Marcos said afterwards that he was young, polite, and almost jealous of the opportunities that Marcos had had abroad. He asked questions about:

1. His departure from Brazil and the details of his arrival.
2. His life abroad and the work he had been involved with.
3. The addresses where he had lived.
4. His ideology.

Question: "Are you a Marxist? What do you think about Marxism?

Answer: "It is a useful instrument to analyze history, but I have some reservations about its philosophical basis."

5. Question: "What do you think about the Brazilian reality in terms of its social, economic, and political aspects?"

Answer: "I don't think anything about it. I've been out of the country for several years.

The interrogator then repeated aloud as he wrote: "Has no opinion about the social, political, and economic aspects, since he has been out of the country for several years."

6. Question: "Do you think that Brazil should continue to tie itself to the western world or do you favor equal distance given the bipolarity that exists in the world today?

Answer: "Equal distance."

7. Question: "Imprisonment: how many times and what were the dates?"

Answer: "Only in the OBAN."

8. Question: "Did you read *Le Monde* and write anything against Brazil? Where?"

9. Question: "Did you attend meetings of the JUC [Catholic University Youth]?"

Answer: "Yes, as a student."

10. Question: "Do you know Ricardo Zaratini Filho?"

Answer: "No."

Question: "Do you know Francisco Batista Duarte? He said he was invited to the Students' Association by you."

Answer: "Yes, while I was in the university."

11. Question: "Do the newspapers abroad criticize the Brazilian government?"

Answer: "Yes, the *New York Times*, the *Washington Post*, and *Le Monde*, which I read."

As they spoke I stared fixated on their legs, fearing that at any moment Marcos might disappear from my sight, a sign that he had been arrested again. Happily, this did not happen, and Marcos and I left in peace.

Many people might ask themselves at this point: Why should we remember all this? To this I respond: It is because we want justice. Justice has never been given to those who were kidnapped, tortured, or killed by the dictatorship. Moreover, I believe it is immensely important that people know what really happened in the dark basements and the torture chambers during those long years. These crimes remain unpunished.

I have spoken with many Brazilians, as well as foreigners, who have asked me why I no longer live in the United States and why I returned to Brazil after so many years. I respond by telling them what Marcos suffered and how we fought to save him. There are some who doubt what I say, while others are surprised and ask to know more. One American woman told me that, after we spoke, she was unable to sleep.

I hope that this book, which has been well documented and which has taken more than three years to write, will convince all of the sad truth about the reality of such cruelty. I hope also that all may know that many, many others were tortured and killed by the dictatorship and that, what is worse, we need only read today's newspapers to see that the torture and killing continues. They are rural workers, street children, homeless, and innocent poor who are made to work as slaves.

Studies and statistics have documented such treatment. Among them, a recent report by Amnesty International regarding the crimes committed here and around the world.

For this reason, I repeat my great hope that the future will bring true justice and independence to the Brazilian people. When will it be?

Marcos continues to fight for his ideals and for the good of all people, without demonstrating hatred or despair even though he was made to suffer so much. He is unselfish and dedicated, but I should allow his friends to speak on his behalf, as a mother is always suspect when it comes to praising her children.

I have, nevertheless, admired his lack of rancor since the beginning, and even after he was released from prison. He did not allow himself to be destroyed by bitterness or by the desire for vengeance.

Marcos must still cope with two consequences of his imprisonment. The first is that his left forearm continues to suffer chronic edema from his wrist to his elbow. His lymphatic vessels in that arm burst after being tortured on the pau-de-arara (parrot's perch). Specialists have since warned that he must avoid any infection in that arm because he has lost the defense of his immune system defenses there. The immunologist Marcos has seen with some regularity has issued a signed statement that the lesion was caused by being tortured. On a few occasions over the past few decades, he has had infections that began in his finger and then spread throughout his entire forearm in the form of red spots and swelling. Only antibiotics prescribed by the immunologist have caused the infection to disappear.

Another consequence of his imprisonment is that his right shoulder still has the scars from being burned by cigarettes. The small toe of his left foot likewise bears a burn scar from receiving electric shocks. He recently fell and landed on his left shoulder. He began to have severe pains and to lose some movement. The doctor who treated him noted that he had also suffered trauma from the pau-de-arara, which had caused a noticeable difference in the height of the left shoulder in comparison with that of the right.

I end here by thanking all who have read this book and by including the words Marcos wrote on the back of a photograph, just a year after his release:

Los Angeles, March 1972
Dear mother:

From beneath this hat
I see the world as it is
Plunging headlong into space and time.
The eye in the dark sees the tragic hours of today
and sheds a shadowy tear.

The eye in the light
Grasps History by the horns
And predetermines the future
Of a new Humanity
That will not die.

Epilogue

NO PATH
FOR THE
RIGHTEOUS
TRAVELER

Marcos P. S. Arruda

TRANSLATED BY

Rex P. Nielson and James N. Green

"TARRY YE HERE, AND WATCH" MATTHEW 26:38

. . .

"I've never met her."

. . .

"I don't know her."

. . .

"I'm just a simple metalworker."

. . .

"Aaaaaaaaaaaaaaaagggggggggghhhhhhh!!!!!!!"

"Jesus Christ, Jesus Christ, Jesus Christ, I am here . . ." The recording of Brazilian crooner Roberto Carlos blasted from the Operation Bandeirantes headquarters, a small, three-story building in the military police compound on Tutóia Street in the center of São Paulo. Tied upside down to a "parrot's perch" by my wrists and knees, I could see an apartment building through the thick windowpane. Buried under the loud music, the cries of the tortured can't be heard by the neighbors. Could Robert Carlos, a man of faith, ever have imagined that his song would be used for such a vile purpose?

During the six hours that I hung from the parrot's perch, I had the privilege of reviewing some of the defining moments of my life. As I swung in the presence of death, it happened almost unconsciously. I was a young man, twenty-nine years old, and I had made some important decisions about my life. One of them was to fight all forms of oppression, although at the time I didn't realize the extent to which my decision would entail confronting social injustice. The military dictatorship that had taken power in 1964 had gradually curtailed all freedom of expression. Its actions culminated with the imposition of Institutional Act No. 5 in December 1968, a presidential decree that shut down the National Congress and marked the beginning of brutal repression against any form of resistance that favored democracy. With their strong sense of freedom, young people reacted vigorously against the government's repressive measures, which seemed to affect every aspect of life in Brazil: wage freezes, political persecution, silenced artists, media censorship, and eventually the creation of illegal prisons, systematic torture, and the murder of political prisoners. The nation's youth believed that another Brazil was possible. Thousands decided to abandon their white-collar jobs and middle-class lives to work in factories, where, identifying with the daily privations of the profession, they educated workers to organize and fight for human dignity and their rights as citizens. I was one of these imbedded activists.

From the point of view of the technocrats that came to power in 1964, the military dictatorship symbolized the future. From a human and social perspective, it represented the past. Those who had seized political power had been financed by Brazilian and foreign commercial interests. President Lyndon B. Johnson, who escalated the war in Vietnam, backed their efforts. The U.S. ambassador Lincoln Gordon and his Military Attaché Vernon Walters were directly involved with the generals in plotting the military coup. I couldn't help but join others seeking a future of dignity for our country and our people, who had already faced 500 years of ethnic and financial oppression.

The military leaders' greed for power was wed to the Brazilian elite's desire for money and prestige. The rule of law mattered not. They considered their own interests more important than those of society at large. Their actions unmasked Brazil's bourgeois democracy, revealing its underlying authoritarian and hypocritical character.

As I hung from an iron rod, receiving beatings and electrical shocks, I felt death approaching. The experience confirmed my disgust for the military's egocentric system of government, the culture of hypocrisy, and the politics of despotism. In my mind's eye, a series of images arose before me: I saw the mounted police of Carlos Lacerda, the governor of Rio de Janeiro, pressing against student demonstrators, forcing us towards soldiers armed with machine guns on the steps of the City Hall in Cinelândia. I saw pictures of Magalhães Pinto, the bank owner and Governor of Minas Gerais, and Ademar de Barros, the Governor of São Paulo, who both supported the coup. They were standing steadfastly beside General Castello Branco, the first of five generals to act as president during the military regime. I saw the image of Roberto Campos and Delfim Netto, the Finance Ministers who justified wage freezes and turned over our natural resources to foreign companies. I saw the miles of fence in Mato Grosso, protecting the enormous estate that was said to belong to Delfim Netto. I saw the faces of my impoverished coworkers from the metallurgy factory, along with their wives, children, parents, and grandparents who had aged prematurely because of the harsh working conditions. I saw the anguished faces of young mothers migrating from the arid Northeast in search of water and life. I heard in my mind the protest songs of Sérgio Ricardo, Chico Buarque, João do Vale, and Geraldo Vandré, lifting the spirits of millions. I saw the blank pages in the newspapers, which had been censored by reactionary military leaders. I saw the sad smiles of my coworkers recently released from prison where they had been threatened with death "if they should continue to provoke violence within the unions and in the streets." Then I saw the devastating scene of the peasant's funeral in the play *Morte e Vida Severina* in which the actress delivers the haunting line, "This grave, measured in inches, is the best payment you received in life!" And then the tender face of my grandmother appeared. And her voice said, "My son, take care. You shouldn't put your life at risk, but I trust you. You are like your grandfather, Belisário Penna, who also fought for justice. He was removed from his government post and imprisoned, but he remained a worthy patriot!" I remembered the affectionate embrace of my father the last time I left Rio, just weeks before my arrest: "I'll pray for you, my son; I'm proud of your courage."

Retreating in time, I recalled my happy childhood when my parents were still married. My mother had always been interested in my personal development. She had me start taking piano lessons when I was five years old. My love of music eventually became the strongest force in my life. I was carried away by the piano—a complete instrument that combines melody and harmony, body and soul, intellect and emotion, matter and spirit. My greatest desire was to be a pianist and composer, but two factors interrupted this dream. One was that I lost access to a piano. With five children, my mother and father didn't have enough money to buy or rent a piano, so I practiced at my Aunt China's house. The only time available for me to practice happened to coincide with the only time my cousins had to receive visitors. I was effectively prevented from going over to play the piano.

The dissolution of my parents' marriage also interrupted my musical aspirations, albeit indirectly. Although my parents could no longer communicate, my father didn't want to leave, so my mother slept in the living room. She slept there for four years, hardly speaking to my father. My unconscious fear at the age of fifteen was that I would lose her love too led to my decision to join the priesthood and renounce everything that seemed pleasurable. I thought my decision would save my parents' marriage. Driven by my pain, I decided to adopt a celibate life and renounce music. If my parents' separation had been my first trauma, I was living my second one now. Naked, I flinched from the electric shocks. The fusion of these two traumas flashed before me. Again I felt the anguish of seeing my father incapable of regaining my mother's love.

My mother's insistence that I not go to the seminary was useless. During the months prior to my departure to the Anchieta Seminary in Friburgo, an unexpected friendship kindled between us, which confirmed for me that I had not in fact lost her love. We took art classes together. We went to the movies, and we talked about the reasons she and my father had separated. Nevertheless, the emotional turmoil surrounding their separation had left deep wounds. Continuing to resist her requests to stay in Rio, I left for Friburgo.

At the seminary in Friburgo I learned discipline, and I had the illusion of being closer to the Divine. There, and later at the Novitiate in Itaici, I discovered a Church whose practice is much more the negation of faith and of the Gospel than I could have ever imagined. But it was also a place where I made lasting friends.

A renewed insistence from my mother that I apply for a scholarship to study in the United States led me to leave the seminary for a time. I was accepted as a foreign exchange student and assigned to the McCartin family in Chicago, Illinois. The year I spent there when I was sixteen years old was one of unforgettable discoveries, thanks greatly to the host family that welcomed me so warmly.

The electrical shocks I was given broke my train of thought as I heard a cry burst from my chest. I saw the wild eyes of the torturers. They smoked, laughed, and asked questions, while watching my body contort in pain caused by the army field generator they had adapted to deliver the shocks. It was a U.S. invention, brought to Latin America by the CIA at the service of the U.S. Army as an interrogation instrument.

Those who resisted the military dictatorship knew they could be arrested, tortured, and perhaps killed. Many of my fellow workers, whose courage and life of honest labor and poverty was an example to me, had been arrested by the police or the military and were already back at the factory fighting for a free Brazil. They gave me the strength to face my torturers without admitting where I really lived, which saved Hasiel, Leo, and Luisa, friends who shared a house with me in Vila Baronesa. I even was able to save João, with whom I went to work every day at the Sofunge plant, and with whom I met at night and on weekends to plan educational and organizational activities with our fellow workers at the factory. With these friends I had many conversations about wages, working conditions, politics in Brazil, our rights, and the need to join the union and participate in meetings, even those controlled by the labor leaders who supported the military government.

In 1958, my mother decided to move to the United States to find work. I was still living there at the time, working part-time selling newspapers outside a church in Chicago and as a painter at St. Ignatius High School where I studied. With some of my savings I helped my mother buy a tape recorder. She used it to train herself as an interpreter and work in New York. Soon afterward, she changed jobs and moved to Washington, D.C., hoping that she could bring all of her children to live with her eventually. Meanwhile, I returned to Rio where I was reunited with the rest of my family and returned to Friburgo to rejoin my class in the Catholic seminary. My mother couldn't believe that I still wanted to continue there.

I thought to myself, "If poor workers who have almost no formal education continue the fight, then I, with all my intellectual, moral, and spiritual training have no right to give in to despair. I have to resist."

My spirit was also influenced by the heroism of the Vietcong. With very few weapons, they mounted a fierce resistance against the armies of South Vietnam and the United States, which were armed with the most sophisticated equipment and financed by the wealthiest country in the world. The Vietcong were fighting *for the same cause that we in Latin America stood for: the right of our people to the sovereignty over our own land, economy, and path to development. The Vietcong who were imprisoned were also subjected to torture. Many, if not the majority, were executed in a cowardly fashion by those who captured them. It was clear to me, as I hung from the parrot's perch, that I was not alone, although the torturers told me that I was, trying to demoralize me. There were millions like me throughout the world, and their strength nurtured my determination not to remain silent.*

In Itaici, I dedicated myself entirely to the search for spirituality. I studied philosophy, Latin, and Greek. Life at the seminary was intensely regulated and designed to probe one's religious commitment. For example, I had to work for a month as a bricklayer's assistant on the construction of the College's chapel. It was my first experience as a laborer.

At the seminary, everything seemed to be a sin. I once even confessed to the Father Superior that I had given in to temptation and read the vulgar writings on the door of the laborers' bathroom. To discipline our juvenile impulses, the priests instituted self-imposed torture, such as the use of whips, cilices, and kneeling on wooden benches in the cafeteria during meals, and publicly declaring "mea culpa." Latin was the only language we were permitted to speak among ourselves, except during hours of recess.

Another religious probation consisted of a two hundred kilometer pilgrimage on foot through the rural interior of the state of São Paulo. Tarcísio, another seminarian, and I each carried a small bundle of clothes. We slept in churches and hospitals, asking for food and water along the way, serving the sick, and announcing the Gospel to those who would receive us. This journey through the Brazilian countryside led me to question my decision to become a priest. I decided to leave the Novitiate and the Society of Jesus.

The torturers wanted to know the real names of my friends. They questioned me insistently about where I was living. I needed more strength to resist. My body broke out in a cold sweat. The pain seemed to have no end. I thought of Jesus, tortured with a whip and a crown of thorns, forced to carry the cross through the city to Calvary, and then hung there with nails through his hands and feet. I thought of his sacrifice, his courage to die for love of humanity. How could I choose to collaborate with torturers to save my small life? A voice within me said, "But if you save yourself, you will be able to continue the fight later on. Dead, you will fight no more." Then a different voice answered, "You don't want your friends and coworkers to experience this pain. If you die, your example will nurture the courage of many others. If you don't die, you will continue to fight with a dignity that will mark your entire life. Resist!"

Leaving the Novitiate was a death of sorts for me. Not only was it a radical change in my life's direction, but also it meant saying goodbye to friends I had joined along the path of faith and hope. On the day I left, I was prevented from embracing my friends. In the calm of the early morning, I was forced to depart as a criminal, and I walked to the train alone. But I carried as my luggage the rich traditions of Latin, Greek, and philosophy, as well as a disciplined way of studying, working, and living.

When I arrived in Rio, my family met me with great joy. I felt perplexed and almost frightened by my newfound freedom and the possibility of a new profession. Later, I felt this same frightening sensation of freedom when I was released from prison. At first I was tempted by the piano as a career, but something led me to look to the field of science. I was determined to study oceanography. I wanted to combine my passion for nature with my desire to participate in scientific research in the service of human knowledge. At the time, I could not foresee the radical redirection my life would take while at college.

A new group of torturers arrived. Their fury to extract information continued. Time was a key factor—the longer it took to obtain the names and addresses of dissidents, the more likely it was that they could escape, and the authorities would lose the opportunity to break up organizations fighting against the dictatorship.

I enrolled at the university and, as planned, began studying science. A friend of mine had encouraged me to study geology and then later to specialize in oceanography. The study of physics, chemistry, biology, and mathematics opened new possibilities for my intellectual development. The four years I spent at the National School of Geology (NSG) transformed my life. College marked my passage from the romantic world of adventure and the mystical life of the soul to the rational world of science. My life became consumed with my studies of philosophy, geology, and history, the critical thought of Karl Marx, Friedrich Engels, Vladimir Lenin, Antonio Gramsci, and innumerable other revolutionary thinkers. One of the authors who has remained present in my mind for decades, who bridged the two worlds of science and faith; past, present and future; material and spiritual, was Pierre Teilhard de Chardin, the French paleontologist and mystic who was impassioned by nature and by the search for the essence of life. I found in his work ideas that resonated with my inquisitive and uneasy spirit.

At the NSG, among members of the Catholic University Youth movement and within the National Union of Students, I developed new and lasting friendships. During this time, I began to participate actively in the Catholic University Youth. It was through this organization and student activist events that I discovered what is commonly called "militancy." This phase of my life represented liberation from my politically conservative heritage. It signaled an opening for indignation, for critical thought, and for transgression. My first lesson was to realize that we must choose appropriate methods to achieve the ends we desire.

During this time I began to transcend my concern over purely spiritual faith, esoteric in the negative sense of its focus on a God disconnected from the world and our day-to-day life. I was profoundly moved by the critical situation in Brazil, so I took up the challenge of studying geology as a mission. I wanted to learn how to discover and extract oil and minerals in order to place them in the service of society. While in school, I learned about the reality of transnational corporations that continued the brutal colonization of Brazil and the rest of Latin America that the Portuguese, Spanish, and English had begun centuries earlier.

As a student leader with the Catholic University Youth, I discovered that the poor *favela* dwellers who lived near my home in Botafogo suffered not from "destiny" or the "will of God" but from a long tradition of colonial exploitation. I had received an intellectually rigorous education, but it was one that had completely ignored contemporary social conditions. My conscience had in fact been *formed* to serve that world of inequality, and it was difficult to break free from that way of thinking. Such a change in perspective and consciousness required great effort, and I had to move beyond the conservative and reactionary heritage I had received from my family, from the private schools I had attended, and from the Catholic Church.

The abdication of President Jânio Quadros in 1961 and the subsequent military intervention in order to prevent Vice-President João Goulart from taking power was my first political trial by fire. I was caught up in the passions of that time, and I participated intensely in the student movements spreading throughout the country. My involvement also meant that I had to face a crisis within my own middle-class, conservative family. At home I had constantly heard sermons against nationalism, populism, unionism, and the discourse of leaders like President Getúlio Vargas, Vice-President João Goulart, and General Lott. By the time I was twenty or twenty-one years old, I knew I needed to break with my past. This parting of the ways with my family led me to find a new connection between my faith and my place in society. It also led me to join the people's fight for a better world without oppression, domination, injustice, and inequality.

I enthusiastically joined the movement to defend the Constitution and João Goulart's right as the elected Vice-President to assume the Presidency. I went to demonstrations, and I argued with people in my family and at school as part of the attempt to broaden support for those opposed to a military coup. My involvement, however, came at a cost. I lost my friendship with Professor Othon Leonardos, the director of the NSG, who was also the director of the German corporation Mannesmann Mining Company. I had passed the university entrance exams with flying colors and was elected president of the student organization at the NSG; however, my social and ethical metamorphosis soon qualified me as "communist." This, in turn, inspired me to study the writings of Karl Marx among others. If I was convinced that everything I did was aligned with my Christian faith, then what were the commonalities between this faith and communism?

During this period, I went through personal changes as well. Soon after graduating, I got married, but unfortunately the relationship lasted only two and a half years. We separated after we moved to São Paulo.

The new "team" intensified their brutality. Captain Albernaz, the most sadistic of them all, had led the group that arrested me. The new group leader was Captain Homero and later Captain Dauro. A few days later, while being held in the Military Hospital, I was visited by Captain Faria. I gave the new team the address of my ex-wife's aunt and uncle's home, where I visited from time to time, and once more I gave them the nicknames of my friends from the factory. When they saw that I continued to resist and refused to give any new information, they decided to increase their cruelty. They took a bare electrical wire and ran it from my ear to one of my nostrils and to my lips and tongue so that the path of the electric shock would be that much longer. The shock extended from my head down to my left little toe. Then they doused me with water to intensify the pain. They burned my shoulder with lighted cigarettes, and they slapped my bare right buttock so hard I felt as though they were burning me. Their beating left a swollen blood clot that took months to go away. Bleary and exhausted, I didn't even have the strength to cry out from the pain. I had lost all feeling. My body broke into a cold sweat, and I realized that I was again close to death. If I had once felt a small death at the separation of my parents, this was going to be my second death, perhaps the definitive one. I unexpectedly felt great courage—an emotion that came from the thought that I was giving my life for the freedom of Brazil and for those who were suffering. My death would help nourish the fight against oppression. I would be a seed from which other flowers would bloom. When they finally brought me down from the parrot's perch, I was nearly dead. But I was still conscious. One of the torturers took the iron rod that had suspended me and hit me in my testicles to wake me up. Then he put his gun in my mouth and cocked it, saying that I was going to die right there. But suddenly my body began to shake and the convulsions wouldn't stop. My tormentors quickly gathered and were obviously concerned, "And if he dies in our hands," one of them said, "this will look dirty. And we haven't even done anything like what we usually do to these fucking commies! Call the doctor!"

In 1963 I helped to create the National Executive Secretariat of Geology Students, linked to the National Union of Students, and I was its second president. The next year, I spent my summer vacation working in Minas Gerais with the Mineral Policy Group. I helped to organize a large national meeting that was called, "Minerals Don't Have Two Harvests." Held in Belo Horizonte, the meeting featured the presence of Miguel Arraes, the governor of Pernambuco, and Almino Afonso, the Minister of Labor under the Jânio Quadros administration. The objective of the meeting was to work with union members, political activists, and professionals from various fields to put forward a proposal for the creation of Minerobrás, a type of

Petrobras for minerals that would regulate Brazilian mining and place it at the service of the country's development.* I believe that this was one of the factors that motivated the military takeover in 1964. Minerobras threatened the direct interests of some U.S. companies that later backed the dictatorship. They owned rich iron and manganese reserves in the states of Minas Gerais, Mato Grosso, and Amapá.

Shortly after the meeting in Belo Horizonte, the military coup was carried out. Because of my participation in promoting Minerobras for the sake of national sovereignty, I had to spend several weeks in hiding. After it seemed that danger had passed, I returned to the university and graduated at the end of 1964. Our graduating class was considered "subversive" by the dean, so we were not allowed to choose our graduation speaker. We had wanted the leftwing educator Paulo Freire or the economist Celso Furtado, but the dean denied both requests. We ended up being denied a graduation ceremony.

After I graduated, I was unable to find work as a geologist in Rio de Janeiro. My wife and I ended up moving to Petrópolis, a little over an hour from Rio. I spent the next year working there with a project involving aerial photographs and geologic interpretation. The project required mapping large regions, analyzing the geological structures, and identifying areas favorable for mineral occurrence. A year later, I was let off because of some financial problems within the company. I looked for another job, but in Rio de Janeiro few would hire me. Eventually I submitted my résumé to the National Department of Mineral Production. Francisco, a former colleague from college who worked there told me, "Of all the candidates who applied, you had the best résumé, but the American who directs the Copper Project vetoed your name." While I sought a job in geology, I began working as a translator for Vozes Publishing House. My wife and I returned to Rio de Janeiro, and I continued translating. I also began volunteering with a literacy project for low-income teenagers and adults, employing the Paulo Freire method. I had met Freire in Recife some years before. About this time, I was invited to work as an assistant to the director of the hydrology section of the National Department of Sanitation. I loved the field of hydrology,

* *Editor's note.* Petrobras is a state-owned oil company that was founded in 1953 after massive popular mobilizations to nationalize the oil industry.

but the constraints created by the authoritarian bureaucracy profoundly irritated me.

They gave me a shot that caused me to sleep for several hours. When I regained consciousness, I was lying on the ground. Urine had pooled by my side. They had clothed me. My left leg was limp and wobbly. My little toe was burned from the electric shocks. I heard the snores of more than one of the torturers sleeping in a side room. Only then did I realize that I hadn't died yet. The terror of returning to the parrot's perch overwhelmed me. Intermittently, my body continued to shake with incessant tremors. My middle fingers were involuntarily curved inward. The nerves of my face also continued to pulse out of control. I could only see through a small slit in my right eye. The proximity of death was very real. Scenes from my life continued to play out before me.

The year was 1967. Besides working with the National Department of Sanitation and volunteering with the literacy program in Rio de Janeiro, I had become a member of *Ação Popular* (Popular Action), a leftwing political group that worked to overthrow the military regime. I was given the responsibility of convincing intellectuals to speak out for human rights and against the dictatorship. One day the police knocked on the door of my father's house, where I had lived until I graduated and got married. My father innocently told them where I was living, but fortunately the police didn't find us at home. I was warned ahead of time and left with my wife for São Paulo, where an old friend of mine, Frei Betto, who was a member of the Dominican seminary, helped familiarize me with the mega-city. I soon began working again with a literacy project involving underprivileged workers. I got a job teaching geological sciences at Santa Cruz High School, and I worked for a time with the magazine *Realidade*. To make ends meet, I also gave private lessons and tutored. We lived this way until my marriage ended. After we went our separate ways, I gave up everything and began a job as a factory worker for Sofunge, a company controlled by Mercedes Benz. My motivation was to help other workers learn to read, write, and fight for their rights.

Terror was my strongest emotion. My body was crippled, and the idea of suffering the same brutality again haunted me. At the same time, I felt I could suddenly see time clearly. As terrible as those moments were, I knew they would not last forever—either I would die or I would be released. The most important thing was to live each moment as honorably as possible, with the spirit of a warrior of light and peace. Those who tortured me would not be the depository of my hate—that belonged to the social system that had made them, that had so brutally disfigured them. What they were doing to me and to others they were actually doing to themselves as members of the human race.

Where would I be a month from now? A year from now? Thinking of how I would like to feel in a year, in ten, if I survived, gave me the will to endure the present. Life answered my question with a generosity that did not include many of the other prisoners and victims of torture. A month later, I would be in a military hospital undergoing treatment and preparing to be interrogated and tortured again. A year later I would arrive with my mother in Washington, D.C., and begin eleven years of exile.

My simple realization of the flux of time and the importance of each moment gave me renewed strength. Nonetheless, I was unable to sleep any longer. I considered trying to escape, but I knew they would kill me. I was being held inside a military compound and was too weak to stand. My body convulsed regularly and would continue to do so for the next eight months. When the torturers awoke and checked on me, they saw that I remained prostrate on the ground, my body shaking with intermittent convulsions. They decided to take me to the military hospital. At this point my left leg, which had suffered electric shock, had hardened like a piece of wood. When they tried to put on my shoes, they were unable to do so, even after hammering with their fists and kicking at my twisted foot, trying to force it into the shoe. I was taken in handcuffs by ambulance to the hospital. There they placed me in a cell in the soldiers' infirmary. The cell was guarded by some of the torturers from Operation Bandeirantes, who delighted in telling me with their sadistic smiles: "You haven't escaped us. We'll get you once again."

I remained there for a month and a half, alternating between interrogation sessions with the torturers and medical treatment.

I worked for two years in the factory. It was a hard experience that taught me a lot, especially through my relationships with the other workers and union members. They taught me about friendship, sincerity, trust, and a culture different from my own. I experienced greater culture shock when living and working among the factory workers than when I lived in exile outside of Brazil. The difference between social classes and educational levels can be greater than the difference between nationalities and languages. This was my view as a geologist who had come from the middle class. One can only imagine the enormous gulf that separates wealthy Brazilians and the urban and rural lower-income classes who barely earn the minimum wage each month.

My fellow workers spoke a semantically different language and had other customs, another aesthetic, and a way of relating to each other that was quite different from my background. I had to readjust my worldview in order to integrate into their world. It was a rich, new experience in culture and consciousness.

Before moving to the working-class suburb of Vila Baronesa, I lived for about a year in an apartment in Perdizes with Pedro Alexandrino de Oliveira, who was like a younger brother to me. Pedro was a bank employee who had joined Ação Popular and had gone to work in a factory in Osasco. The change was difficult for him, and he later left Ação Popular. Then, in an act of extraordinary courage, he joined the Araguaia group, the militant underground arm of the Communist Party of Brazil that organized rural guerrilla activity in the Amazon. Pedro's whereabouts have never been resolved. His mother, Diana Piló de Oliveira, continues to this day to tirelessly fight to preserve the memory of her heroic son and to find his remains.

In Perdizes I met various freedom fighters. Two of them, Manoel da Conceição and Zé Barbosa, became lifelong friends. Manoel had come from the state of Maranhão to São Paulo to receive a prosthetic leg in place of the one he had lost because of police brutality. The police had massacred men, women, and children who had met in a field hut during a religious revival meeting led by Manoel, who was an evangelical pastor. Manoel had been shot several times in the leg by the police and had been thrown in prison without any medical attention until gangrene set in. Only then was he taken to a hospital to have his leg amputated. This was but one of the many crimes of then-Governor José Sarney, who later became President of Brazil and remains the "emperor" of Maranhão. Today Manoel is the founder and energy behind the Center for the Education of Rural Workers in Imperatriz, Maranhão.

Zé Barbosa was a leader of metalworkers in Santo André, in the Great São Paulo area, and was one of the organizers of the massive May 1, 1968, rally in downtown São Paulo. Government repression of the rally was violent, and Zé had to go into hiding. I was responsible for helping him escape. He spent nearly ten years in exile, and we spent four of those years together in Geneva and Guinea Bissau. He now lives with his family near Olinda, Pernambuco.

In November 1968, I obtained a position at Sofunge, a subsidiary of Mercedes Benz, a factory that employed three thousand workers. I moved from Perdizes to a house in Vila Baronesa, a poor community that did not have running water. Although I enjoyed the company of the other workers, I felt the harsh reality of our situation. We were forced to work twelve hours a day. I remember one conversation with my fellow workers.

"The law in Brazil says there should only be eight hours of work a day, plus a ninth hour for lunch. We are working three hours extra!"

"But they pay overtime," someone responded.

"But we are only paid a minimum wage, and the overtime isn't worth the effort. I'm on my own, but João is married and has a little kid. He arrives home exhausted and only has a little time on Sunday to be with his family."

On the third or fourth week of each month, we all ran out of money to pay for transportation to get to work. We would get up an hour earlier to walk, so we could be at our machine by 5:55 A.M. We then walked home, twelve hours later, or later still when we had extra work to complete. Between my work at the factory, the meetings at night, and the weekend visits from my colleagues from Ação Popular, I had practically no time for leisure. Only later did I understand that the difficulties of organizing workers at Sofunge were linked to the problems in the Northeast, the original home of most workers who came to São Paulo without any professional qualifications.

One of my colleagues explained, "I came from Ceará in the Northeast. I lived through a miserable drought. The lack of water and poverty pushed me to São Paulo in the hope of finding a more honorable way to make a living. It's true that Sofunge does improve our lives. We can eat two or three times a day, and I have a paycheck that comes at the end of each month. I have a little rented house and a mattress for my wife and me and our children."

I was forced to stop work at Sofunge when I broke my foot, so I took advantage of my time off to visit my family in Rio de Janeiro. I returned to the factory, and a few months later I began coughing a lot. An x-ray showed that I had an infection in my lung.

On a Sunday morning in 1970, silence filled the military hospital in São Paulo. The soldiers' infirmary was empty. I seemed to be the only soul inhabiting that space. I could see little birds in a tree outside. How I desired to get up and watch them from the window. Suddenly, there was the sound of keys opening the heavy lock that secured the iron door. Two plainclothes officers from Operation Bandeirantes entered. I shivered. One of them quickly approached my bed and roared, "Now you'll see who Adão is, you son of a bitch!"*

He began punching my stomach with both fists. I was prostrate, my body overcome with nervous spasms. My damaged leg was motionless. My right eye was shut, and my left eye was barely open. I tried to protect myself with my arms while shouting for help. My nurse was a nun named Sister Catarina. After a few minutes of terror, the Sister entered. She was indignant. She ordered the two officers to leave and threatened to call the captain, the chief of hospital security. Sister Catarina had not believed that I had been tortured. Although she was kind and attentive, I once heard her say as I regained consciousness after a fit of convulsions, "For him to be here, he must have done something." Now she had evidence that my story was true. "Sister, I can't go on with these torturers guarding my cell. They threaten me every day, and today you've seen what they can do! I need to denounce their behavior to the captain!"

The x-ray had revealed an infection in my lungs.

"Doctor, what do I have?" I asked.

"It's not clear yet, but you can't continue to work twelve hours a day. From now on, you can only work eight hours a day, as the law says."

"But they'll fire me!" I responded both startled and indignant.

"Not if I give you a medical voucher to give to the factory."

I gave the document to the personnel division, and a few days later I was let go. I went to see my supervisor.

"Why are you firing me? Are you dissatisfied with my work?"

He answered, "Not in the least. You are an excellent worker, and we are satisfied. The problem is that you can't work the hours that the factory requires."

"But that is what made me sick!"

---

* *Editor's note.* Adão was the name of one of the two plainclothes officers who attacked Marcos.

"That isn't a consideration. The factory needs employees who can do what is required. Outside every morning there is a line of people asking for work who can do what we want."

They changed my guard. They replaced the torturers with a military police detail of two soldiers. I spent the next month and a half being examined, tested, and treated with anti-convulsive medication. Then one day they sent me back to Operation Bandeirantes. I panicked. I was locked in an office above where the prisoners were tortured. They asked me to write a deposition. My hand still trembled. I didn't have enough motor control to write easily. I remained there for about four or five days.

I was taken from the office to a large room where I was brought face to face with two police officers and, to my surprise, Marlene. She was a woman whom I had met in São Paulo. We had arranged to meet at a restaurant in the neighborhood of Lapa, in the south end of the city. It was there that I was picked up by the police. Now, she looked well. It was clear that they wanted me to reveal information. I thought they were simply going to question me to get me to contradict myself. I was mistaken. It was another session of brutality. As soon as I saw her, I began to speak, "You told them that I . . . ," but I was cut off as one of the officers yelled, "I am the only one who will ask questions here. You will answer, nothing else!"

In her deposition, published in the book Brasil, Nunca Mais *(Brazil Never Again) Marlene recounts that prior to my entering the room, they had told her to get ready to see Frankenstein. Indeed, a month after I had been tortured, I was still in bad shape. My face was somewhat contorted, only one eye partially opened, and I walked with the help of a broomstick. I could barely lift my left leg off the ground, and my stomach and arms shook lightly. She greeted me with an expression of shock and sadness. Marlene seemed honest and courageous, and I felt no anger towards her.*

"For the last two months we've held Marlene in Tiradentes Prison, and she has collaborated with us and told us everything she knew. Her story about you, however, doesn't substantiate what you have told us. If anyone is lying, it is you."

"What I told you was the truth. I have nothing else to say."

They took Marlene from the room. They beat the floor with a wooden club, while she pretended to scream. Back in the room, she didn't look upset. More questions. Silence. When they took her from the room a second time, she let out a piercing scream and returned trembling from head to foot. They were torturing Marlene to force me to speak. I faced two impossible options: remaining silent and allowing her to suffer, or giving the names of others who would be arrested and tortured. In the middle of this desperate situation, we heard a great noise from the stairwell. We were quickly taken to our cells. The team of Captain Albernaz had arrested a new group of young people and needed to torture them immediately.

Back in my cell, I could hear the imperious shouting of soldiers, mixed with the cries of pain of the new prisoners. They received electric shocks and were beaten. It is impossible to describe the suffering and impotence one feels hearing the pain of other healthy and idealistic young people being tortured. It was a Reign of Terror—this time the Terror of the State. I prayed that these young people could connect to their inner strength and resist.

Suddenly there was a soft knocking from underneath my bed. I looked, but I didn't see anyone. Another knock. It was soft but insistent, like someone asking to come in, and it seemed to come from underneath my bed . . .

For two weeks I was out of work. I experienced the impotence of every worker who feels unjustly mistreated and without resources to fight back. Because of the polluted air in my area of the factory, I had become sick. For having received medical treatment and been required to work "only" the hours established by law, I was fired, without any compensation. Outside the factory, I woke up early each morning and went to visit other factories in the area to try to find work.

Unable to find another job at a factory, I went to a vocational training school to begin a course to become a quality control inspector. Shortly thereafter, I found a job with a small metallurgy factory that distributed specialized steel products. The firm was called Stora, a subsidiary of a large transnational Swedish company of the same name. As an assistant, I was responsible for overseeing the transportation of heavy metal loads within the factory. My time there was short lived, however, because the company complained about my request not to work extra hours in order to attend the training school, and I was fired.

Out of work, I began again to look for a new job.

"You, you, and you, come in. The rest of you, take off; there are no more positions!" I was one of the rejected at *Metal Leve* (Light Metals) Corp.

that morning. I walked downcast alongside another rejected worker. He was weeping.

"For the last month, I've spent all my money just looking for work, and I haven't found anything! If I pay to take a bus home, I'll have no money left to buy food for my family. If I buy food for my family, then I can't look for work. I'm desperate."

Unable to help him, I felt great compassion and grief. We separated, and I wished him well. This was the life of the metalworkers and their families in the most advanced city in South America. Modernization led by the military dictatorship, based on profit and the accumulation of national and transnational capital, came at the expense of exploiting workers and accelerating environmental destruction. This process gained momentum in the 1970s. As the economy grew and expanded, so did the gap between the rich and the poor. I lived this brutal reality with my fellow workers. I gained concrete experience that supported my indignation about capitalism. This served to strengthen my resistance to torture when my time came.

"Are you there?" It was the voice of Marlene, coming through the outlet at the bottom of the wall under my bed. Was she alone? Was there a soldier by her side? Had microphones been installed to record our conversation? I couldn't trust her.

"Yes, I'm listening."

"I want to tell you how devastated I am about having caused your arrest. I was tortured for four days before I gave in. I don't have words to ask you for forgiveness. Three other people also were arrested because of me."

I felt the deep pain that afflicted her. She was being sincere. Tears ran down my face.

She continued, "I want you to know that I've gotten the word out that you are being held by Operation Bandeirantes. The people from Ação Popular already know, and your family does too."

This news was like a ray of sunlight. They knew where I was. My friends would have left our house, destroyed any leads about their whereabouts, and informed my family about my imprisonment. My mother would be able to publicize my situation in the United States. The soldiers won't be able to disappear me so easily.

"One more thing," Marlene continued. "Tomorrow they will probably torture us again. And they might torture me to get you to talk. Marcos, even if they kill

me, don't change your story. Be faithful to the end! If you change even a little, they will want more, until they kill you or you tell them what you didn't want to."

She was offering her life in exchange for mine.

"I can't *not* go and meet Marlene," I told Hasiel, a man of great courage and a faithful friend. He insisted that it was too risky because many of the people she was connected to had been arrested. I was wearing a pair of light blue, threadbare pants, an old shirt, and worn shoes. I was carrying only a little slip of paper, which contained weekly appointments. On the way to meet Marlene, I bought a copy of the *Estado de São Paulo* newspaper. Marlene, a dentist from Santa Catarina, wanted to leave the underground organization *Resistência Democrática*, also known as REDE, and join us in Ação Popular to work in a factory. There was no time to lose. The group that she belonged to was being decimated by the dictatorship's repressive apparatus. She needed a place to hide.

Hasiel walked me to the bus stop.

"Don't go, Marcos," he said in his friendly way.

"If she hasn't already been arrested, she'll be lost, with no where to go."

"But you don't even have a place for her to hide."

"You're right, but I can tell her that I'll continue looking for a place, and we can set up another meeting in case I find a place for her to stay."

Hasiel was right. If I had found a place for her to hide . . . But our attempts to find something for her, even a temporary location, had been frustrated. I thought about that courageous woman. She was less than forty years old, and we had taught literacy classes together. Now she needed our help.

Two police thugs approached me. One spun my chair around and the other hit me with a "telephone"—a special blow in which he cupped his hands and simultaneously slapped both my ears. I nearly fainted on impact at the violence of the blow. I was dizzy and had no strength. The younger of the two soldiers was more aggressive.

"Talk right now, or we're going to finish you!" He slapped me violently on my face. I didn't say anything.

"Let's get out of here," he said to the other cop. The two left the room, but the thin walls allowed me to hear their conversation.

Epilogue

"What can we do to make this son of a bitch talk?"

When I heard their frustration, my heart filled with courage. So, they were the powerless ones. So, they were feeling defeated because they couldn't bend my spirit.

Back in my cell, I felt even more renewed because they had not tortured Marlene again. I was intrigued. There was no one in the room next to me. I imagined that she had been returned to Tiradentes Prison. The next day, I was brought to another room.

"I am a doctor and a general," said the white-haired man with an educated air. He contrasted strongly with every other person I had met in that bleak environment.

"I have some questions to ask you, and I want truthful answers," he said. "Serve him some coffee," he ordered the officer by his side. He continued, turning back towards me, "We know that you have a profession. You are a geologist. How is it that you are working in a factory for minimum wage?"

And then, as if to test me, he began to ask questions about tectonics and sedimentary basins. Then he began to talk about politics. He wanted to know why I was in jail and in such bad shape.

"I was badly tortured."

"There is no torture here. It must be something else," the general replied dryly.

He said that he had all of the evidence he needed to be convinced that I was a member of Ação Popular. He was being polite, but I knew that this was an old police tactic. Generally, a prisoner's interrogators are changed. Different interrogators are used for different purposes: one flatters you, treats you well, and gives you the impression of being a friend. Then he leaves, and his violent replacement comes in. In this case, the conversation went on until I decided that it should end, since we couldn't come to an understanding.

"I've never heard of this group REDE that you are talking about. I am a member of Ação Popular. We fight against social inequalities that are absurd in a country as rich as Brazil. We fight so that the riches of the country benefit all Brazilians and not just the elite in Brazil and in the United States. You say that this fight is a lost cause, that all I need to do is collaborate so that I can be released and go on with my 'normal life,' but as a geologist, I don't see the world or its history through the lens of the here and now. For me, our lives are made up of decades, history is measured in millennia, and the earth in billions of years.

And everything is constantly changing. You can maintain control for a few years, but looking ahead, you have already lost, for Brazil will not support this for much longer."

The general lost his temper and yelled, "You are more dangerous than a hundred armed guerrillas!" Then he turned to his assistant saying, "Take him away and put him on bread and water."

They put me in a cell on the ground floor with three other prisoners, giving me only bread and water. I remember little of the conversation I had with them. These were times of general distrust, and I was traumatized. Conditions in the cell were dismal. There was no bathroom, and the bars of the windows opened to the patio. It was freezing cold.

That night I had another convulsion. I had gone too long without the anti-convulsion medication that I had been instructed to take three times a day.

I got off the bus and looked around to see if there was a suspicious person or group waiting for me. I turned toward the corner, and from that angle I could see, across the street, the restaurant where I was going to meet Marlene for lunch. She was standing at the door. When she saw me, she waved. I responded. Immediately, I felt a pistol barrel jammed into my side. Two cops grabbed me by my arms, one on each side. I dropped the newspaper I had been holding under my left arm. They forced me to pick it up. I saw that I had no time to hide the small slip of paper that had my weekly activities listed. I put it in my mouth and tried to swallow it. My mouth was dry from the stress. They immediately began to punch my stomach and squeeze my throat to force my mouth open.

Then they shoved me into an old blue and white Rural Willys jeep. Marlene sat on the seat in front of me beside Captain Albernaz. I sat between two policemen, who were pointing their machine guns at me. Everyone wore civilian clothes. As the jeep sped off, Captain Albernaz said, "Marlene, show him what's in store for him." She didn't turn her face but merely lifted her two handcuffed wrists. Her hands were thickly swollen, bandaged, and covered with dried blood, like two enormous blood blisters.

We finally stopped inside the Military Police Compound on Tutóia Street. I was pushed out of the jeep, and Captain Albernaz delivered me to a team that was waiting for me in the courtyard. I was taken to the entrance of a two- or three-story building in the middle of the compound, where I was forced up the steps inside. No one said anything. We entered a room, and I could see in the back two sawhorse benches with an iron bar across the top. Near the wall there was a phone with exposed wires waiting for my body.

"Take off your clothes, shoes, socks, everything!" they yelled. There were four of them—a captain and three henchmen. All were in civilian clothing. I was tied upside down to the rod, and only after they had begun to administer electric shocks did they finally begin their interrogation.

Five or six hours later, I was lowered, half-dead, from the parrot's perch to the ground. My life seemed to flash before me, preparing me to pass over to another existence.

In that moment, life seemed like a road with two forks equally open to me: one pathway led to death, and the other to survival.

"Your grandma is here at the hospital entrance. If you would just tell us one thing, your address, she can come and see you. Look, I brought a note she wrote to you."

A sergeant was speaking to me. He didn't bother to hide his name, Sardinha, which was embroidered on the left pocket of his uniform. He was black, nice, and treated me well. I was paralyzed and lying on a hospital bed. I could not move my left leg and the muscles were atrophying. One of my eyes was swollen shut, and the other was half-closed. My body shook intermittently, as it had since my torture began. My right shoulder had burn marks from cigarettes. My wrists were still swollen, and the wounds made by the cords that tied me to the parrot's perch were raw. The abrasions were made worse by the pull of gravity during the hours I spent hanging from the metal bar.

The note from my grandmother encouraged me to collaborate. She must have written what they had dictated to her. After the initial "My dear child," she had written, "Your war is over. Collaborate with the police, and I will be able to see you and end this separation that has given us so much pain."

"I have nothing to tell you besides what I have already said," I responded. My grandmother was not allowed to see me. Only later would they let my family see me, two people at a time. They never let me see my lawyer, Técio Lins e Silva. Moreover, every time one of the revolutionary organizations kidnapped a foreign ambassador to demand the release of political prisoners, I was once again held incommunicado, my family couldn't visit, and my cell door was locked tight.

During the brief period when I was allowed visits, I shared a cell with a young Argentine named Hugo Miguel Moreno, who had recently arrived from Italy. After I had undergone torture during interrogation with Marlene, they returned me to my cell in a semi-conscious state. It was during this period that they brought Hugo to my cell in the hospital. He had likewise been tortured and suffered from renal hemorrhaging that worried the military doctors. I don't know how many days I spent in what I was later told was a state of amnesia. I recall, though, being treated for it with electric shocks on two occasions.

However, I gradually improved to the point that I could communicate. At this point I received the inspiring news that my mother was there to visit me. It was an indescribable feeling to be embraced by her. New life pulsed through my body, strengthened by the loving presence of the person who had brought me into this world. In her embrace, we both cried out of joy and gratitude for life. The captain responsible for hospital security had the decency to leave us alone, and I told my mother everything I had lived through. I also asked her to deliver a message that Hugo had written to the Argentine Consulate, asking for help to get out of prison.

The visits of my grandmother, my father, and my sisters filled me with emotion. Weeks would pass, and then suddenly I was cut off from the outside world again. Why was I refused the right to be visited by my lawyer? The law was applied arbitrarily as yet another means of terrorizing opponents of the regime. And the military were afraid of outside witnesses to the ill state of my health after torture.

Finally, I received word that I was being transferred to Rio de Janeiro. The news filled me with tremendous joy. I was going to be freed at last from the clutches of my torturers.

I was transferred in an armored ambulance lying on a stretcher, so I couldn't see out of the windows. When the ambulance finally parked inside of a building, I was blindfolded and taken in handcuffs into the main building of a compound. It was the Military Police Compound on Barão de Mesquita Street in Tijuca, Rio de Janeiro. After I was photographed and closely examined, I was taken to the Military Hospital at Triagem, a district of the city, which wasn't far from the Military Police headquarters. Inside the hospital I was locked in a small white room and placed under heavy security. The only furniture in my room was a cot and a small bedside table. Despite the shadow of fear that still rested on me, I was at least closer to my family. Surely, it would be easier for them to get permission to visit me. From my new hospital cell, I could no longer hear the cries of others being tortured.

Through the high, barred window of my room, I could see some branches from a mango tree and hear the birds early in the morning and late in the afternoon. In the silence of the rising and setting sun, their chirping and warbling created a sensation of infinity. I especially loved listening to the soft wind in the trees and the song of the *sabiás*, a common Brazilian songbird. My imagination was like a canvas on which the diverse melodies combined and recombined to make colors and forms that were always new and beguiling. These pleasantries, nonetheless, couldn't prevent me from soon realizing that I was entombed in a white coffin, completely alone.

Instead of being released from the immediate fear of more torture and reaching a place where I could hope for freedom, I was submerged even deeper in dark solitude and isolation. No one spoke to me for several weeks, not even the attendant who brought me my food. When I greeted him as he entered with the tray, he remained silent or murmured an unintelligible response. Finally, after several weeks, a good and honorable man named

Valter who worked the weekend shift began to listen to me and respond to my story. He was tall, thin, and dark. He was missing teeth in his crooked mouth, and he had a sensitive heart.

During the months I stayed in the Military Hospital, my trust in him grew, and Valter became a precious friend. He seemed to understand the reasoning behind our cause and silently expressed his approval. Little by little, he began to vocalize his indignation over the fact that he witnessed so many young political activists arriving at the hospital with their bodies broken and their minds terrorized by the possibility of further torture. Valter had seen the coldness of the military doctors who treated these young men and women just enough so that they could be returned to their torturers. He also spoke about the injustices that he and other workers had suffered.

On the other hand, the director of the hospital ward was a gloomy and contradictory figure. His name was Doctor Boia, and there was a rumor in the hospital that he was in reality a dermatologist. He was fat, middle-aged, and unkempt. At the same time, he played the mandolin and liked serenades. I never had a conversation with him although he was in charge of the prisoners and prepared them to return to be interrogated.

Many different types of prisoners came through the infirmary, from convicted political activists to common criminals. Each day, we had the right to spend half an hour in the sun out on a small patio that separated our ward from the women's ward. Valter was the one who told us about the female political prisoners. He was also the one who delivered my first note to them, written on a small paper I had torn from one of the few books allowed in the prison.

Through Valter, I met Estrella. She was twenty-one years old, recently married, and had carried out political activities with workers in Volta Redonda. She had been tortured, and when she said she was pregnant, they kicked her in the stomach. She came to the hospital with a hemorrhage in her uterus. In one of the notes we exchanged, we agreed to try to talk through the windows of our cells at night when no one was around. We spent many nights in the calming darkness talking about our lives, politics, loves, and hopes. The windows were high, but we could hold on to the bars. I would stand on my bed and look out across to the other side of the patio where she could see me from her cell. She told me that there was another prisoner in the same cell who was pregnant. Only after eleven years of exile was I able to meet her cellmate, Irony Bezerra, who was bravely dedicated to her efforts on behalf of the working class. She was pregnant with her daughter Adriana, who is the current coordinator of the Center for Community Action (CEDAC) in Rio de Janeiro, which her mother co-founded in 1979. In her hospital cell, Irony could not stand because of her pregnancy, so I never saw her until I returned to Brazil in the 1980s.

Estrella was a courageous young woman. She knew that she was being treated in order to be returned to her interrogators. One day at the beginning of December, Valter came to talk to me. He was worried. "They've come to take Estrella back!" he said. "Do you have anything to send to her?" I hurried to write a note to encourage her and give her some comfort. I had only a pencil tip and a scrap of paper, but I expressed my hope that she would be freed. I gave the note to Valter and asked him to cheer her up, since it was likely that she was being returned to DOI-CODI. Afterwards, I sat leaning against the bed frame and playing *The International*, the revolutionary anthem, on the contralto flute that my uncle and godfather Guiga had arranged to have delivered to me. I put all of my feeling into the melody, and while I played, tears ran down my face.

Soon after, I received a visit that is sad to recall. A bishop sent by the Apostolic Nuncio appeared at my door. He was accompanied by the Director General of the hospital. A chair was placed beside my bed and the Director General left. I explained to the bishop my motives for working as a laborer. I told him that I wanted to feel the workers' suffering and help them defend their rights. I told him stories about the violence that I and other political prisoners had suffered while in jail. I also advised him that I had been cut off from my family and been denied the right to see a lawyer.

"I did not come for this," the bishop said coldly. "I came to learn whether you will leave here and tell the world what happened to you or whether you will be quiet and mind your own business."

I was shocked and perplexed. This man who claimed to represent God was there to deliver a message from the bastards who were holding me! Unmoved by the story I had told him, he had only one message: conform, be quiet, forget. "I do not belong to this church," I thought to myself.

Epilogue

A few days before Christmas, Valter came to tell me that he thought I was going to be freed. A little later, a nurse brought me an order to prepare my things to leave. He gave me a package with my old clothes and shoes. I put my things in a small bag. They included the few books my grandmother had sent. Before putting my shoes on, I hid the two or three notes that Estrella had given me inside my socks. My heart raced with expectation. I gave Valter a long hug and looked once more at the trees and birds that had been with me outside the bars of my window. I never wanted to return.

I was transported in handcuffs back to the Military Police Compound. A police captain and two officers, all in civilian clothes and armed with machine guns, rode with me. They treated me as usual. There were no signs that I would be freed. (Later, I was able to identify the blondish captain as Gomes Carneiro, one of the cruelest torturers of DOI-CODI.) They blindfolded my eyes with a hood. The handcuffs were the kind that tighten with each movement. The jeep bounced along, and the handcuffs painfully squeezed my wrists with each bounce. My hands quickly began to swell. By the time I was told to get out of the jeep, they were throbbing. They removed my handcuffs and handed me the end of a broomstick, which they used to lead me along. They made me remove my shoes, but not my socks. After they carefully searched me, they led me upstairs. Estrella's notes were still hidden in my socks, and they reminded me symbolically of her presence, strengthening my spirit for whatever might happen. I was locked in a cell with painted green tiles that extended to the ceiling. It was the last of eight cells in the hallway. Again I was alone. "What have they brought me here for?" I asked myself. "They said that I was going to be freed, and here I am, as though I am about to be tortured again."

It was a macabre Christmas Eve. One prisoner after another was taken from his or her cell only to return beaten and tortured. Some couldn't even walk, and the soldiers had to drag them back in. Throughout the night, we listened to the piercing cries of those being tortured. No one knew who would be next. The next day, once again deprived of my anti-convulsive medication, I had another attack. They decided I should leave.

I was taken by ambulance back to the infirmary-cell of the Military Hospital. Those who had seen me leave, expressed their surprise at seeing me return. An employee came and told me that my family had called to wish me a Merry Christmas. I asked, "Did you know that I was not going to be released?"

"No. But I think it must have been because of another kidnapping, and they think that your name might be on the list of the prisoners to be exchanged."

"I am certain it is not," I answered. "As I have always said, I was never involved with the organizations that have done the kidnappings."

Another month went by. Finally, on the first of February, I left the Military Hospital for the last time. They took me to the Army Ministry building next to the Central do Brasil train station and led me to a room where I met Colonel Mello.

"You are going to be freed, but you'll have to report to me once a month. You will tell me about each person you have contact with and everything you have done."

I was free, but closely watched. I imagined my future life, constantly observed by their spies, afraid to meet with my friends because of the risks that they would face by being associated with me. I remained silent.

"We know that you are a born subversive. Your mother is as well. Watch out for yourselves. That's all I have to say. If you don't like Brazil, then leave."

Later, accompanied by my father, I had another conversation with this same Colonel.

"You studied with the Dominicans, right?"

"I studied with the Jesuits."

"It's the same thing. And you met with the Dominicans. This explains your subversive nature. But there's another thing. Arruda is the name of a plant, so you must be Jews, and therefore subversive."*

---

* *Translators' note.* In Brazil, it is widely thought that sixteenth-century Portuguese Jews, who had converted to Christianity to escape persecution, chose common plants and animals for their last names.

Epilogue

This was the mind-set of the Brazilian military that could not understand how political activists that opposed the dictatorship could love their country and its people. They didn't take me home, nor did they give me money for a taxi. They only allowed me to make one telephone call.

"Grandma? I am at the Army Ministry. They're going to let me leave right now. I'm going to take a taxi home, but I don't have any money. Could you please get some money ready to pay for the taxi when I arrive." She exploded with joy. "Oh, my child, our prayers finally have been answered!"

In spite of her joy, I felt insecure and intimidated. What would happen to me when I walked out into the street? Would they merely kidnap me again, as they had done to Márcia Savagé and Marijane Lisboa, two other members of Ação Popular? It had required a hunger strike by all of the prisoners being held on Ilha Grande by Cenimar, the intelligence arm of the Navy, before they were released. The hunger strike had attracted international attention and exposed the brutality of the military regime. If they kidnapped me again, no one would know for sure what had happened to me. I had no feeling of freedom as I stepped out onto the pavement of Presidente Vargas Avenue. I tried to flag down a taxi as quickly as possible, constantly fearful that this was all a trap.

But even so, my emotions soared. I was like my dear sabiá who sang outside my window at the hospital infirmary. My cage door had been opened, and now I could fly. The sky was no longer crisscrossed with bars. I could hardly take it all in: the streets, the cars, the people walking around, surely ignorant of the terror that so many of us were experiencing. There I was, unaccompanied. After having spent nine months under constant surveillance, without the right to move, and paralyzed by the always imminent prospect of torture, I was unaccompanied, headed toward the home of my grandmother and Aunt Elza.

The taxi took me to Voluntários Street in Botafogo without incident. As I got out in front of our building, I noticed a car parked across the street with two plainclothesmen watching me. I rang the doorbell. It was a celebration, everyone hugging amid smiles and tears. Yes, I was free.

After nine months, the impossible dream of freedom had become a reality. What a mysterious gift life was offering me now. My body, torn apart by torture, began the road to recovery. Finally, I could fully open both eyes. The tremors in my face and abdomen disappeared. My left leg slowly healed. The little toe on my left foot, which had turned black because of the electric shocks applied to it, regained its normal color. The two cigarette burn marks on my right shoulder turned into light scars. Some things required more time to heal. My left forearm continued to be swollen for quite some time. An immunologist later told me that the lymphatic system of my forearm had been destroyed. Any cut or wound in my hand or fingers would lead to an infection, and the entire arm would swell. I still limped a little and had trouble focusing my attention for more than a few minutes at a time. I was also instructed by my doctors to continue taking anti-convulsive medication indefinitely. This medicine had an uncomfortable side effect. It caused frequent mental fatigue. Learning to focus my attention became one of the greatest challenges of my therapeutic process.

The loving embraces of my family were a reward for having insisted on living and enduring my tribulations with dignity.

I finally met my lawyer a few days after I was freed. Técio Lins e Silva was one of the brave lawyers who defended political prisoners without remuneration. During the administration of General Médici, the military set aside the law. I had spent nearly nine months from the time I had disappeared without any contact with friends or family and without access to legal defense. Then, three months after my release, Técio brought me news that my name had been included in a legal suit brought against members of Ação Popular. Suddenly, the risk became very real that if I were present at the trial of this case I might be imprisoned again. My subsequent decision to leave Brazil came because of pressure from my family and my friends in Ação Popular, who sent me a message insisting that I go abroad to be able to continue my neurological treatment and physical therapy.

I had been attending yoga classes for a couple months, and I walked daily on the sands of Copacabana and Ipanema to exercise my damaged leg. Before joining the workers in Sofunge, I had practiced yoga postures and deep breathing exercises. I had learned to recognize the benefits that this exercise produced throughout my entire being. Now, I was taking advanced classes that led me to discover even more profound dimensions of yoga. On the other hand, my anti-convulsive medicine gave me the sensation of feeling distant. I was convinced that my inability to concentrate was linked to this treatment.

I didn't want to leave Brazil. I had only just been reunited with my family and friends, and my fellow Brazilians. I wanted to continue fighting for justice. Estrella and so many others were still imprisoned. How could I abandon them and selfishly think only of myself?

The airport was full of loved ones: comrades from the Catholic University Youth and Ação Popular (those who weren't in hiding), my university colleagues from the School of Geology, my lawyer Técio, and Hugo, who had been the director of the Dominican Convent. This wave of affection and energy gave me the courage to leave. I didn't know when I would see my family again. Only my mother and my sister Tiana, who lived in Virginia, would be near me. From the small window at my seat, I could see everyone waving in the distance. Seated by my side, my mother tried to cheer me up by talking about the health and security I would experience in the United States. Although I was happy to be by her side and was enchanted by the full moon that shone on us from heaven, my heart was filled with sorrow. The United States was a country that had supported and financed the military coup in 1964. President Nixon and Secretary of State Kissinger continued to sustain the dictators who ruled Brazil and who had opened our land to exploitation by companies from Europe and the United States. I was leaving behind not only the people I loved and my country, but also those who were fighting for a free Brazil.

How would I continue this fight from far away? My sadness and confusion were profound. Only later would I understand that my flight into exile was the fourth flight to freedom that life was giving me.

EDITOR'S POSTSCRIPT

Maria Penna Sattamini, Marcos's grandmother, quietly passed away at the age of 101 in 1997.

Clemildo Lyra de Arruda, Marco's father and a retired Greek and Latin teacher, also died in 1997.

Elza de Britto Pereira, Lina Penna Sattamini's sister and Marcos's aunt, became an actress in her 60s and appeared in Brazilian films, television commercials, and soap operas.

Miguel Arruda lives with his wife, children, and grandchildren in Rio de Janeiro.

Cristiana Arruda still resides in Berkeley, California, where she has been active in the women's movement for many years.

Martinha Arruda works as an interpreter and is the mother of two children, Suiá and Yama.

Mônica Arruda has worked as an environmental educator, and lives in Rio de Janeiro.

Marcos Arruda built a house on a steep hill in Rio de Janeiro where he lives with his wife, Catherine, and their son, Pablo, who is an accomplished musician. Marcos continues to be active in the struggles for economic justice and social equality.

Lina Penna Sattamini, now retired, owns a cozy apartment downstairs from her son Marcos. She misses the United States.

BIBLIOGRAPHY

Alves, Márcio Moreira. *A Grain of Mustard Seed: The Awakening of the Brazilian Revolution*. Garden City, New York: Anchor Doubleday Press, 1973.

Alves, Maria Helena Moreira. *State and Opposition in Military Brazil*. Austin: University of Texas Press, 1985.

Amnesty International. *Report on Allegations of Torture in Brazil*. Palo Alto: West Coast Office, Amnesty International, 1973.

Archdiocese of São Paulo. *Torture in Brazil*. Translated by Jaime Wright. Edited and with an Introduction by Joan Dassin. 1st ed., 1986. Austin: University of Texas Press, 1998.

Arruda, Marcos. *Transnational Corporation: A Challenge for Churches and Christians*. Geneva: Commission on the Churches' Participation in Development, World Council of Churches, 1982.

——. *External Debt: Brazil and the International Finance Crisis*. Translated by Peter Lenny. London and Boulder: Pluto Press in association with Christian Aid and the Transnational Institute, 2000.

Arruda, Marcos, John Cavanagh, and Daphne Wysham. *Beyond Bretton Woods: Alternatives to the Global Economic Order*. London and Boulder: Pluto Press; Washington, D.C.: Institute for Policy Studies; Amsterdam: Transnational Institute, 1994.

Bartoli, Amalia, Roger Burback, David Hathaway, Robert High, and Eugene Kelly. "Human Rights . . . 'In the Soul of Our Foreign Policy.'" NACLA *Report on the Americas* 3, no. 1 (March–April 1979): 4–11.

Black, Jan Knippers. *United States Penetration of Brazil*. Philadelphia: University of Pennsylvania Press, 1977.

Boal, Augusto. *Hamlet and the Baker's Son: My Life in Theatre and Politics*. Translated by Adrian Jackson and Candida Blaker. London: Routledge, 2001.

Calvacante, Pedro Celso Uchôa and Jovelino Ramos, eds. *Mémorias do exílio, Brasil 1964–197?*. Lisbon: Arcádia, 1976; São Paulo: Editora e Livraria Livramento, 1978.

Della Cava, Ralph. "Torture in Brazil." *Commonweal* 62, no. 6 (April 24, 1970): 135–41.

———. "Reply." *Commonweal*, 62, no. 14 (August 7, 1970), 378–79, 398–99.

Erickson, Kenneth Paul. *The Brazilian Corporative State and Working Class Politics.* Berkeley: University of California Press, 1977.

"Estratégia para matar o terror." *Veja* (November 12, 1969): 22–28.

Green, James N. *We Cannot Remain Silent: Opposition to the Brazilian Dictatorship in the United States.* Durham: Duke University Press, 2010.

Hall, Clarence W. "The Country that Saved Itself." *Reader's Digest* 85 (November 1964): 135–59.

Huggins, Martha K. *Political Policing: The United States and Latin America.* Durham: Duke University Press, 1998.

Huggins, Martha K., Mika Haritos-Fatouros, and Philip G. Zimbardo. *Violence Workers: Police Torturers and Murderers Reconstruct Brazilian Atrocities.* Berkeley: University of California Press, 2002.

Kinzo, Maria D'Alva Gil. *Legal Opposition Politics under Authoritarian Rule in Brazil.* New York: St. Martin's Press, 1988.

Langguth, A. J. *Hidden Terrors.* New York: Pantheon, 1978.

Langland, Victoria Ann. "Speaking of Flowers: Student Movements and Collective Memory in Authoritarian Brazil." Ph.D. diss. Yale University, 2004.

Leacock, Ruth. *Requiem for Revolution, The United States and Brazil, 1961–1969.* Kent, Ohio: Kent State University Press, 1990.

Marighella, Carlos. *For the Liberation of Brazil.* Middlesex: Penguin Books, 1971.

Morris, Fred B. "In the Presence of Mine Enemies." *Ramparts* (October 1975): 57–70.

Page, Joseph A. *The Revolution that Never Was: Northeast Brazil: 1955–1964.* New York: Grossman, 1972.

Parker, Phyllis R. *Brazil and the Quiet Intervention, 1964.* Austin: University of Texas Press, 1979

Pereira, Anthony W. *The End of the Peasantry: The Rural Labor Movement in Northeast Brazil, 1961–1988.* Pittsburgh: University of Pittsburgh Press, 1997.

Power, Timothy J. "Brazil and the Carter Human Rights Policy, 1977–1979." M.A. thesis. University of Florida, 1986.

Quartim, João. *Dictatorship and Armed Struggle in Brazil.* London: New Left Books, 1971.

Rabe, Stephen G. *Eisenhower and Latin America: The Foreign Policy of Anti-Communism.* Chapel Hill: University of North Carolina Press, 1988.

———. *The Most Dangerous Area in the World: John F. Kennedy Confronts Com-*

munist Revolution in Latin America. Chapel Hill: University of North Carolina Press, 1999.

Sattamini, Lina Penna. *Esquecer? Nunca mais . . . (A saga do meu filho Marcos P. S. de Arruda).* Rio de Janeiro: OR Produtor Independiente, 2000.

Serbin, Kenneth P. *Secret Dialogues: Church-State Relations, Torture, and Social Justice in Authoritarian Brazil.* Pittsburgh: University of Pittsburgh Press, 2000.

Skidmore, Thomas E. *Politics in Brazil, 1930–1964: An Experiment in Democracy.* 2nd ed. New York: Oxford University Press, 2007.

————. *The Politics of Military Rule in Brazil, 1964–85.* New York: Oxford University Press, 1988.

U.S. Congress. House of Representatives. Subcommittee on International Organizations and Movements of the Committee on Foreign Affairs. *Torture and Oppression in Brazil.* 93rd Congress, 2nd session. December 11, 1974. Washington, D.C.: Government Printing Office, 1974.

U.S. Congress. Senate. Committee on Foreign Relations. Subcommittee on Western Hemisphere Affairs. *United States Policies and Programs in Brazil: Hearing before the Subcommittee on Western Hemisphere Affairs of the Committee on Foreign Relations.* 92nd Congress, 1st session. May 4, 5, 11, 1971. Washington, D.C.: Government Printing Office, 1971.

U.S. Congress. Senate. Subcommittee of the Committee on Appropriations. *Hearings on Foreign Assistance and Related Programs,* 93rd Congress, 1st session. January 25, 1972. Washington, D.C.: Government Printing Office, 1972.

Veloso, Caetano. *Tropical Truth: A Story of Music and Revolution in Brazil.* Translated by Isabel de Sena. New York: Alfred A. Knopf, 2002.

Von der Weid, Jean Marc. *Brazil, 1964 to the Present: A Political Analysis, an Interview with Jean Marc von der Weid.* Montreal: Latin American Editions, 1972.

Weis, W. Michael. *Cold Warriors and Coups D'état: Brazilian-American Relations, 1945–64.* Albuquerque: University of New Mexico Press, 1993.

INDEX

LINA PENNA SATTAMINI worked for many years as a freelance interpreter for the U.S. State Department. She is the author of *Esquecer? Nunca mais: A saga do meu filho Marcos P. S. de Arruda* (2000).

MARCOS P. S. ARRUDA is the coordinator of Instituto de Políticas Alternativas para o Cono Sul (Policy Alternative for the Southern Cone Institute), where he has worked for twenty-three years. His research focuses on economics and education. He serves as a consultant for social movements, local governments, and the ecumenical movement, and teaches at the International Peace University and other schools.

JAMES N. GREEN is professor of Latin American history and Brazilian studies at Brown University. He is the author of *We Cannot Remain Silent: Opposition to the Brazilian Military Dictatorship in the United States* (Duke, 2010), and *Beyond Carnival: Male Homosexuality in Twentieth-Century Brazil* (1999). He is the editor (with Ronaldo Trindade) of *Homossexualismo em São Paulo e outros escritos* (2005) and (with Ronald Polito) of *Frescos Tropicos: Fontes sobre a homossexualidade masculina no Brasil, 1870–1980* (2004).

REX NIELSON is a doctoral candidate in Portuguese and Brazilian studies at Brown University. His current research project examines literary representations of socially rooted authoritarianism during Brazil's military dictatorship.

Library of Congress Cataloging-in-Publication Data
Sattamini, Lina Penna.
[Esquecer? Nunca mais—. English]
A mother's cry : a memoir of politics, prison, and torture under the Brazilian military dictatorship / Lina Penna Sattamini ; edited and with an introduction by James N. Green ; translated by Rex P. Nielson and James N. Green ; epilogue by Marcos P. S. Arruda.
p. cm.
Original Portuguese version published: Rio de Janeiro : Produtor Editorial Independente, 2000.
Includes bibliographical references and index.
ISBN 978-0-8223-4718-7 (cloth : alk. paper)
ISBN 978-0-8223-4736-1 (pbk. : alk. paper)
1. Arruda, Marcos P. S. de (Marcos Penna Sattamini) 2. Political prisoners—Brazil—Biography. 3. Torture victims—Brazil—Biography. 4. Political persecution—Brazil—Case studies. 5. Brazil—Politics and government—1964–1985. I. Green, James Naylor, 1951– II. Arruda, Marcos P. S. de (Marcos Penna Sattamini) III. Title.
HV9592.5.A77S2713 2010
365'.45092—dc22 [B]   2009049956